HAWAI'I
A SENSE OF PLACE
ISLAND INTERIOR DESIGN

HAWAI'I
A SENSE OF PLACE

ISLAND INTERIOR DESIGN

MARY PHILPOTTS MCGRATH

WITH KAUI PHILPOTTS

AND PHOTOGRAPHER DAVID DUNCAN LIVINGSTON

MUTUAL PUBLISHING
HONOLULU, HAWAI'I

Written by Mary Philpotts McGrath and Kaui Philpotts
Designed by Cindy Turner, Turner & de Vries, Ltd.
Principal photographer, David Duncan Livingston
Produced by Lloyd Jones
Special project assistant, Hi'ilei Dye

Archival photographs made available by
The Bernice P. Bishop Museum

With special thanks to
Martin & MacArthur Enterprises, Ltd.

ISBN 1-56647-739-5
Library of Congress Catalog Card Number: 2005927295

First Printing, October 2005
1 2 3 4 5 6 7 8 9

Mutual Publishing
1215 Center Street, Suite 210
Honolulu, Hawai'i 96816
Phone: (808) 732-1709
Fax: (808) 734-4094
Email: mutual@mutualpublishing.com
www.mutualpublishing.com

Printed in Korea

CONTENTS

PREFACE

Among the gifts of living in Hawai'i is the privilege of enjoying and reveling in the unique diversity of our people and the extraordinary beauty and richness of the respective historic cultures found here. This inspiring and insightful book speaks to modern day Hawai'i's cultural heritage and its transformation into a seamless artistic blend as it merged with the gentle and spiritual host culture of the Hawaiian people.

Respected interior designer Mary Philpotts McGrath has teamed here with her friend and fellow family member, lifestyle feature writer Kaui Philpotts, to trace the roots of contemporary Island style, showing from its beginnings in Native Hawaiian and missionary dwellings, how it developed and remains timeless to this day. Hawai'i's architects have been directly affected by and responsive to our wonderful climate, while drawing inspiration from both the East and West. The authors trace and discuss these influences and origins, address specific architectural features such as entryways, pitched roofs and deep lānais and refer to unique furnishings such as the beloved all-purpose pūne'e.

They consider the contribution of Hawai'i's multiethnic mix to the islands enduring style, ending with today's most creative and beautiful manifestations of this legacy. They then show you how to apply specific design principles in your own spaces and finally allow you to celebrate with them in a joyous, family-affirming way.

Kaui began working on the project several years ago as a way to tell Mary's design story and show others how to infuse their own homes with a Hawai'i "sense of place." In the process, she learned much about how to use natural island motifs in everything from floral designs to vibrant color and filtered light. She was able to articulate the recurring themes of family, hospitality, lasting value and respect for the environment. Both women pulled upon their part-Hawaiian heritage and richly diverse memories, to give this book real authority and heart.

Fifty years ago, Mary Philpotts McGrath was groomed by the world-class art department at the University of Hawai'i. Well-known artist and professor Kenneth Kingrey was her mentor, always expecting the highest standards of design—unencumbered by trendiness and over-embellishment. She often drove her neighbor, art scholar Dr. Gustav Ecke, to the Mānoa campus and found this time with him to be invaluable to her understanding of art history and classical Chinese furniture. Among her other influential teachers were the scholars and artists Jean Charlot, Ed Stasack, J. Halley Cox and Harue McVay.

Those years at the University of Hawai'i formed Mary's philosophy that culture and art are at the backbone of good interior design. Throughout her career she has mentored emerging artists, craftsmen and designers, encouraging them to integrate what they do seamlessly with architecture. Like all artists, Mary approaches living spaces as she would a blank canvas, using the same high standards passed on to her by that group of blue-ribbon professors who taught that "only the best survive the measure of time."

George Ellis

FOREWORD

Hawai'i ~ A Sense of Place is a celebration of family. Unbounded hospitality and unabashed love of tradition are traits shared by most kama'āina families. The reader will find this typically Island attitude reflected throughout this book compiled by my sister, Mary Philpotts McGrath.

The Flanders girls, Alice, Mary and Judy, collectively known as "Almaju," were raised in O'ahu's lush Nu'uanu Valley in a Hawaiian-style house that had many of the elements captured on the following pages. Our feet were stained black with mud from trapping crayfish in the stream and picking gardenias by the armful in the backyard. Our Nakasan raised us on Japanese food, our aunts provided Hawaiian and Chinese treats and our father produced a perfectly roasted prime rib with Yorkshire pudding for every major occasion. Our beautiful mother composed haunting melodies on one of two grand pianos and our grandmother, who couldn't cook, would occasionally boil water for tea and enthrall us with Hawaiian legends. Our family lived a happily eclectic, sometimes eccentric lifestyle in which artistic endeavor and a quick wit were blatantly nurtured. Our Hawai'i family and extended family numbers in the hundreds and we are in touch often.

As she assembled a design collage that reflects both her discerning eye and her Island soul, this book provided Mary with an opportunity to celebrate her own family values. Her home, "'Āhuimanu," is the venue for family gatherings and a refuge for visiting friends from around the world. Hospitality radiates through the house with softly playing stereophonic music, magnificent garden-gathered floral bouquets, and breakfast, lunch, or dinner for any number of guests whipped up in a magic minute. Mary and John have opened their home and gardens on numerous occasions for family weddings, special celebrations, and charitable events.

Many of the designers, artisans and homeowners featured in this book are family and friends of family. Mary has acted as tutor, mentor, and promoter of young local talent, including her children, her nieces and nephews, and family friends. She has always been extremely generous in providing professional opportunities to others, thereby insuring that a Hawaiian sense of place will continue for future generations.

Aloha pumehana,
Alice Flanders Guild

INTRODUCTION

What comes to mind when you say Hawai'i? Vacations, warm beaches, and the twang of steel guitars. Hawaiian style is more often associated with Tiki god trinkets, surfer shorts, and bright florals than with its reality.

The way Islanders actually live, when they live well, is often unknown. True Hawaiian style is based on informality and the melding of cultures. Located in the middle of the Pacific, between the U.S. mainland and Asia, and with cultural ties throughout the South Pacific, our style is a variation on many themes.

A few years back, when we were working on the concept for the Hawai'i Convention Center near Waikīkī, Hawaiian scholar and business mentor George Kanahele and team leader Don Goo assembled the designers on the near-vacant site; we ate our plate lunches sitting beside the Ala Wai Canal. There, in the shade of a tree, as we watched the activity out on the water, we struggled to find a phrase that described exactly what we were trying to create—then it came to us. We wanted the design to embody "a sense of place." We wanted those who came to the Center to know that they were not in Chicago or San Francisco or San Diego. There had to be no doubt that they were in our Islands.

As a designer, my job has always been to connect people to this environment and create for them "a sense of place," of living harmoniously with our climate and people. Fads and fashion, while acknowledged, are never primary to Island design. Instead, I try to create spaces with lasting value and timelessness, to pull from you what you already know about the way you want to live.

The best contemporary Island interiors use design elements essentially unchanged for hundreds of years, showing respect for these elements and for the people who inhabit the rooms. We use what's already here, then mix it up with treasures found in our travels and our daydreams—items we respond to instinctively. It's often what we choose to put into our spaces, rather than the actual structures, that determine contemporary Hawaiian style.

I believe that creating an interior is a collaboration between those who will live in the home and the artists and craftsmen who will help fill it. I like to approach a space the way I was taught in art school to approach a canvas. The goal is to create beauty by balancing all the elements. In the 1970s and 1980s, Hawaiian interior design seemed to lose its way as developers built mega-resorts and homes with European marble fountains and tightly sealed, air-conditioned interiors. Homes were built to lot boundaries, and gardens reflected the design tastes of landscapers rather than the occupants. Gone were the backyards of mangoes and Meyer lemons for chutney. Gone were the flowers and leaves used in arrangements throughout the home. There was no way to smell the ocean, listen to birds sing, or feel a gentle breeze. Gone was our sense of place.

Today, we look back for design inspiration to a more "Hawaiian" time, when our home style first developed and grew. In the 1930s, 1940s, and 1950s, an aesthetic unique to the Islands flourished. Designers and architects stopped merely copying American and European styles. Instead, they incorporated elements from Polynesia, such as the high-pitched roof, which allowed warm air to escape, and rooms with walls that disappeared, opening onto outside lānai. There was the sense of belonging to the Islands, of knowing where you were. Asian elements, such as Japanese lacquer boxes and Tang Dynasty horses dripping with sancai glazes, were used in Western ways to grace tabletops. Shoji doors and sliding pocket doors carved with Island foliage divided spaces.

Hawaiian interiors have a tactile quality. No matter how sophisticated, there is always a nod to nature with wood, stone, bamboo, grass cloth, and textured fabric. We love the use of native and natural materials—both old and new.

These pages will give you ideas for layering your rooms on your own. You will become more sensitive to how an Island designer "paints a room with light," using slanted shutters and bamboo blinds. You will learn how to make rooms flow, in an unstructured way, from the inside out and back again. There are lessons here for everyone, no matter where you live. Hawaiian living is a state of mind. At its best, it's living with the spirit of aloha—with harmony and affection for others, with cool breezes, bare feet, and the smell of flowers.

Mary Philpotts McGrath

My house will stand on the side of a hill . . .

Where the birds can sing

and the storm winds cry.

A flagstone walk with lazy curves

Will lead to the door . . .

And the door will squeak as I swing it wide

To welcome you to the cheer inside.

From *Vagabond's House* by Don Blanding

ORIGINS

When you look at the beginnings of Hawaiian design style, the timeless quality may not

be immediately evident. Nevertheless, it is there—in the use of natural materials, such

as lava rock and native woods, to the pitched roof and open lānai which reference the

original grass house. We look at the pūneʻe, or communal bed, which has survived many

incarnations, and the use of rattan and surplus materials.

THE ENTRY

Call it a "sense of arrival," that tingle of excitement that runs through you as you approach a place that promises comfort and sanctuary from daily cares. The best homes anywhere have this aura. A tropical Island home is no different.

Sometimes this sense comes from the land itself, the 'āina, but more often it's man-made, created by the owners to welcome all visitors to their door—a way of saying, "E komo mai"—come in and relax. Join us in our home.

The grand homes of Old Hawai'i, those built at the end of the 19th century and in the early years of the 20th, were known for long, gracious driveways, often lined with royal palms. You drove in past pillars of stones gathered from the closest river or cane field, past hedges of pale hibiscus, tangled night-blooming cereus, and a banyan or two.

The house might lie behind a deep lānai that encircled its front and sides. The cool darkness offered relief from the relentless sun and the kaleidoscope of colors outside. Not all Hawai'i houses were this grand. More modest dwellings were built up off the ground to allow air to circulate underneath and cool the interior. They had hedges of hibiscus or panax, and in the backyard were fruit trees dominated by the ever-present mango.

Below: The graceful driveway at the Purvis home on Noela Place at the foot of Diamond Head, circa 1966.

Right: The same gracious feeling continues past mature shade trees and lush foliage at this Kāhala home. It was originally designed in 1930 by the owner David Larsen with the help of a local draftsman.

Most of those old estates have long since been subdivided into smaller lots. The price and value of land have risen; the boundaries have moved in. Yet designers still work at making an arrival statement. It just requires more cleverness. Without the land to convey grandeur, they split pathways that meander and turn, giving you new view planes.

No vast, undulating lawn with a view of the sea? Layer your foliage with varying shades of green. Create visual treats by adding sculpture or oversized ceramic or stone urns to a garden bed, or introduce a water feature. This can be as unassuming as a stone pot filled with water lilies, or as spectacular as an infinity pool and waterfall. Then light it all in the most dramatic way possible.

Smaller spaces require you to visit the surroundings with your eyes rather than your feet. Entering, the sense of welcome, of "E komo mai," remains.

Top: The drama of this contemporary Asian gong, made of koa wood by Martin & MacArthur and designed by Shawn Moynahan, adds to the ambiance.

Bottom: Sunlight bathes a vibrant hybrid hibiscus blossom in a Hawaiian garden.

Opposite: Chinese garden "moon" gates were the inspiration for this contemporary treatment of an Island-style entrance.

Above: Classic Japanese forms influenced this entrance to an old 'Aiea Heights home.

Opposite: Rich wood and oversized doors give this entrance a dramatic "sense of arrival." The large pot filled with tropical leaves and pods found along the roadside was designed by Mary Philpotts and adds to the excitement of the interior. Architecture by Tan Hock Beng and Kurt Mitchell.

This page: Coral building blocks were used throughout this Honolulu home built in the 1930s. The theme of "coming from the land" is always strong in Island design.

Top left: The timeless quality of this contemporary home is enhanced by the stone path and ti garden designed by the team of Lois Nottage, Jean Thomas, Ricky Towill, and Leland Miyano. A welcoming pot of foliage sits to the right of the door.

Top right: Chinese guardian dogs and a stone wall lead the way into this Asian-inspired home on Black Point Road in Kāhala.

Below: A solid hardwood door was custom-made for this new Honolulu home by artisan-craftsman McD Philpotts. The Marquesan design represents the owner's passion for Polynesian tattoo motifs.

Top: Detailed sketch of monstera leaves by Georg James.

Right: A door intricately carved with monstera leaves opens into an entry hall. The simple Chinese altar table holds a vase of tropical leaves and orchids, and a red lacquer Japanese chest from designer Robert Ansteth. The portrait was painted in 1955 by artist Roselle Davenport. Mary Philpotts was the interior designer.

Opposite: This charming back entrance follows a stone path lined with tree ferns and a tangle of foliage. It was foliage such as this that inspired artisans of the '30s, '40s, and '50s.

HOUSES WITH NAMES

From the earliest times, Western-style homes were given names. Perhaps it was a reference to grand mainland residences in the American South or Northeast, or even Europe. But the names given were almost always Hawaiian, and in some way reflected the locale, the land the house was built upon, or special wishes for life in the home. Native Hawaiians, too, felt reverence for place names and for the land's historical use.

Some of the most beloved residences were " 'Āhuimanu" (meaning "gathering place of the birds"), the windward O'ahu home of the Macfarlane family; "Kāluanui," the Baldwin family home at Makawao, Maui; "La'imi" ("awaiting the day"), Albert Afong's home in Nu'uanu Valley; "Niulani" ("heavenly palm tree"), belonging to Harold Dillingham; "Lanakila" ("the hill of victory," the spot on which the battle of Nu'uanu turned), the home of Annie Parke; and the Judd and Wilder family's "Kualoa" near Ka'a'awa.

Songs were written about these homes, and their names sometimes contained the hidden spiritual and erotic meanings Hawaiians loved so well.

Right: This sketch by Georg James of a bronze railing has an abstract bird motif that reflects the home's name, " 'Āhuimanu," interpreted by the family to mean "gathering place of the birds." The design was typical of architect Hart Wood's detailing in the early 20th century.

Below: A bromeliad-filled courtyard flanked by graceful columns provides a welcoming feeling to this historic Nu'uanu Valley home.

Opposite: Mediterranean influences are seen in the stucco walls, curved door, and large earthen pot.

THE GRASS HOUSE

You cannot discuss the Hawaiian home without taking into account the Hawaiian climate. Temperatures in the Islands rarely vary much more than twenty degrees in any direction, and except for spells of "Kona weather," where the winds switch to the south, we enjoy mercifully cooling trade winds.

Hawai'i's first homes were large one-room structures set on a platform and made of thatched pili grass. The high-pitched roof allowed warm air to rise, and life, for the most part, took place on the floor. Even the first Westerners followed the ali'i, or chiefs, and lived in houses such as this. In the early 1800s, they furnished haphazardly with pieces from New England and China, and even some they made themselves from native woods.

The grass house suited Native Hawaiians and their simple, contented lifestyle. They had no need to own or secure their personal possessions, so basic shelter from nature was all that was required.

Missionaries, on the other hand, felt they needed more confined workspaces, as well as storage for tools, books, clothing, and furniture. They found grass houses inadequate, and certainly not what they had been used to in New England. They continued to wear the layered, woolen fashions of the day, buttoned up from neck to toe, regardless of humid weather that hovered in the high 80s.

The houses they introduced were more suited to a climate with snowy frigid winters. The first prefabricated frame house brought to Hawai'i had no eaves to provide shade from the intense tropic sun, and very small windows that made sure every bit of warmth stayed inside. But they did have one thing going for them—the structures were permanent.

Most of these first houses, designed in the style of New England, were made of wood, or a combination of coral blocks mined from nearby reefs and timber beams removed from ships. The Mission Houses complex on King Street in Honolulu provides excellent examples.

Below: Built in 1837 of adobe and grass on the Island of Kaua'i, this classic old Hawaiian house has all the architectural features that have been copied over the years.

Top: This thatched grass house on the Island of Kaua'i, belonging to William Hyde Rice, was photographed in 1900.

Below: The thatched roof used on this oceanside cabana closely resembles the early grass house. It was designed by architect Mark de Reus, the design principal for Hart Howerton.

THE HAWAIIAN ROOF

In the 1920s something remarkable happened to architecture in Hawaiʻi. It became Hawaiian. A style with indigenous inspiration was born. It took a combination of factors—one of which was "good times." The years between 1920 and the beginning of World War II could be described as Hawaiʻi's "Golden Age of Architecture." Because the Great Depression on the mainland reached Hawaiʻi slowly, and much later, the city of Honolulu, and to a lesser degree the Neighbor Islands, found itself in the throes of a building boom.

Leading this boom was an island-born architect named C. W. Dickey. Dickey was joined by other architects schooled in the Beaux Arts tradition that encouraged sensitivity to the use of local historical forms. Several of these architects were from kamaʻāina families, but some were from the mainland. Among them were Hart Wood, Bertram Goodhue, Claude Stiehl, Catherine Jones Thompson, Julia Morgan, Richard Tongg, and Bill Merrill.

Dickey spent twenty years in Berkeley, California, before returning to Honolulu, where he partnered with Hart Wood to build the first of a number of cottages for Clifford Kimball at the Halekūlani Hotel.

The cottages were simple framed structures. What was remarkable were their roofs; they were double-hipped and pitched, held up by columns that echoed the symmetry of the coconut trees outside. The footings were made of lava rock and the lānai were screened to keep out mosquitoes.

Dickey claimed that he had been influenced by the Hawaiian grass house and the Waiʻoli Mission on Kauaʻi built by his grandfather, the missionary William P. Alexander; Dickey and Wood had re-

stored the Mission in 1920. The roof style, so suited to the Hawaiian climate, took off in Island neighborhoods. The Hawaiian roof is as revered today as it was then. Often tapering to cover a deep lānai, the roof, held up by columns, exudes grace and elegance.

The simplicity of this style was ideal for Hawaiian living. Like the grass house, it was both hospitable and unpretentious. Many have since added touches of Asian and Hawaiian decorative motifs to further the look.

New York architect Hardie Phillips worked with Goodhue on the Honolulu Academy of Arts building, which opened in 1928. He believed that elements of Spanish and Mediterranean architecture would be ideal for Hawai'i. Many of the private homes and public buildings constructed at the time, and copied since, have incorporated these styles, with their rough stucco finishes, recessed windows, and wrought-iron railings.

By 1938, public buildings and prominent homes had taken on a different appearance. Plaster-covered stone, wrought-iron railings, and the soaring, dramatically hipped roof attributed to Dickey had taken hold. The more modest houses of plantation families and ranch cowboys were simple, wood-frame board-and-batten structures, with corrugated iron roofs. In the 1930s, kit homes began to appear in neighborhoods like Kaimukī and elsewhere. Many of these were built in the bungalow style popular in California. In the 1950s and 1960s homes took on a decided "ranch style" appearance. The grass house remained fashionable, not as a dwelling, but as an auxiliary building. Sometimes it was the family "party house"; other times it sheltered canoes or boats; and often it was used as a cabana, or a place at the beach to find relief from the sun. Today, we can see the legacy of the simple grass house in any number of outbuildings, from hotel gatehouses to poolside cabanas and Balinese party pavilions.

Opposite top: The Hawaiian-style roof and palm-like columns fit naturally into the environment at "Niulani," the O'ahu home of the Harold Dillingham family.

Opposite center: The old Fagan home on O'ahu, built of stone with a Hawaiian roof.

Below: The pitched hip roof of the Macfarlane home, "'Āhuimanu," built in 1854 on Windward O'ahu, is seen here covered in vines. The home influenced architect Bertram Goodhue's design for the Honolulu Academy of Arts.

This page top: The Wai'oli Mission at Hanalei, Kaua'i, was built in 1841 by the Rev. William P. Alexander and later inspired architects C. W. Dickey and Hart Wood.

Center: The main building of the original Halekūlani Hotel in Waikīkī. The building still stands, but is now surrounded by new highrises.

Opposite: The Hawaiian roof is repeated several times in the additions to this Oʻahu residence.

Left: An ʻōhiʻa post holds up a beam at an entrance to this coral-block home.

Below: The carport of this Nuʻuanu home, designed by architect Philip "Pip" White and designer Mary Philpotts, doubles as a party pavilion. The columns and roof mimic the design of the main house nearby.

Opposite top: A corner of the lānai at the old McInerny home in Waikīkī. Shown is a portion of the hau tree under which Robert Lewis Stevenson is said to have written *The Master of Ballantrae.*

Opposite below: A branch of bougainvillea follows the line of the eave on this house. Hau and bougainvillea have traditionally been trained into hedges and arbors to provide shade and soften the lines of many older Island residences.

Left: An old 'auwai once used to irrigate taro fields has been expanded into a garden pond. On the other end it resumes its original shape to meander through a Nu'uanu neighborhood.

Opposite: This private home on the Kona Coast, designed by architect Shay Zak, has remained faithful to traditional Island characteristics, with a gentle hip roof and wood posts supporting the lānai. The crushed lava lily pond by Mark Blackburn resembles the molten volcanic lava along the coast. The basalt pavers were cut from lava in Kona.

This page: The grove of coconut trees viewed at sunset provides inspiration for other palm forms such as the pillars at the front of the Honolulu home of Senator and Mrs. Joseph R. Farrington, circa 1937.

PAVILIONS

Pavilions in Hawai'i can be as humble as a carport used for family parties, or as elaborate as a full structure with hip roof and sliding-glass doors. Pavilions serve one basic need: They provide protection from nature's harsher elements—the sun and sometimes the wind—while still allowing us to enjoy the outdoors. Rarely seen today are the old-time grass shacks and palm-roofed canoe hales that were once in use in private residences. They now appear most often at resorts.

The hau terrace, a loggia or path made up of a frame of metal poles, with the strong hao vine trained to creep over it, was once a classic element of many Island homes and beachfront restau-

rants. The most famous are at the old Halekūlani Hotel and the Outrigger Canoe Club on Waikīkī Beach. Hau, due to its strength and density, was also used as a barrier along the ocean, and even as a hedge. Other successful creeping vines are the Chinese jade, pakalana, cup of gold, and the Mexican creeper.

Depending upon the homeowner's tastes and interests, pavilions or garden structures vary in style. Lath-and-glass hothouses for orchids and anthuriums are still commonplace. Those who enjoy entertaining build party pavilions or simple gazebos, many of which exhibit an Asian flair. Even traditional Balinese pavilions, often purchased as a kit, have been introduced to the Islands.

Opposite: This pavilion on the Kohala Coast of the Big Island gives shelter from the strong sun while allowing cooling breezes. The roof mimics the Hawaiian style.

This page: The vintage party pavilion, top, and canoe hale, above, have the same open characteristics as the contemporary beach pavilion at left.

THE LĀNAI

Time spent on deep, covered verandas and lānai was a way of life in Hawai'i. Shade trees and awnings were regularly employed to create a sense of coolness. Islanders were driven by two desires: to stay out of the hot sun, and to be in the fresh air. As the 19th century wore on and the non-Hawaiian population exploded, the grass houses clustered around Honolulu harbor were replaced by two- and three-story wooden frame structures that gave the area the look of a Wild West town. Homes were built up Nu'uanu Avenue and into the valley in the Victorian and Greek Revival styles of the time. Builders did make one large accommodation to the climate; nearly all homes had deep, open verandas, called lānai, that encircled as many as three sides of the house.

It was common for the windows between the house and lānai to be completely open to allow for breezes. Only the upstairs bedroom windows had screens. When Kona storms brought rain and wind onto the lānai, furniture and rugs were gathered and piled in a corner and covered with a canvas tarp. Today, the choice is often a glassed-in, air-conditioned lānai. Mark Twain, visiting in 1866, described Honolulu as "that beautiful land, that far-off home of profound repose and soft indolence and dreamy solitude, where life is one long slumberless Sabbath, the climate one long delicious summer day."

Opposite: A stone outside wall and pillars provide perimeters for this modern-day lānai filled with minimal Balinese furniture and a rough table. Potted plants provide a transition to the garden. Interior design is by Mary Philpotts and Belinda Akaka.

Below: Lava rock pillars hold up the extended lānai of this circa 1934 residence. Lauhala mats and rattan furniture are still used on lānai today.

"*In the verandas, enclosed for the most part, and called lānai, the family life goes on. There are cushions and couches, cool braided mats, and writing tables. Often the family dines here and one could sleep on the veranda in comfort. Here callers are received and the household life ebbs and flows in the open air.*"

Hawai'i Nei by Mabel Craft, 1898

Below: Lauhala mats, a koa rocker, and vintage carved koa sofa and chairs are the mainstay of this family lānai of a ranch house in Kona's cool uplands. The architect was Francis E. Skowronski of Territorial Architects, Ltd.

Opposite: Meals are enjoyed at this vintage koa table on the same ranch's lānai. Leaves and flowers for the arrangement come from the owner's yard.

Opposite: Massive 'ōhi'a posts support the extended roof on either end of a Big Island residence. The lānai is minimally furnished, and a pool reflects the posts and sky from many vantage points.

Left: A vintage shot of the Fagan home on O'ahu shows a very deep lānai, with distressed overhead beams, tropical furniture, and Polynesian-patterned fabrics on the pūne'e.

Below: Architect Mark de Reus designed this oceanfront lānai on the Kona coast to face the water and views. He has literally made walls disappear and created a home without boundaries. Interior designer Mary Philpotts placed a Balinese platform bed and rough, colorful Indonesian furniture on the lānai for lounging and gathering.

Rattan and Retro Romance

Rattan furniture, with its curved lines, durability, and splashy tropical-print cushions, made a big impact in sunny locations from Honolulu to Hollywood and as far across the country as Miami. Although it looks very much like bamboo, rattan is made from a plant in the palm family. Most was manufactured in the Philippines, beginning early in the 20th century, but use of the material reached its heyday during World War II and through the 1950s.

California designers Paul Frankel and Don Loper are responsible for many of the innovative rattan designs found both on movie screens of the day and in military homes in Hawai'i. During the 1950s, many people traveled to the Islands aboard Matson's luxury liners, staying at such resorts as the Royal Hawaiian and Moana hotels. When they returned home, they took souvenirs, hula girl lamps, fringed pillows, and Matson menu covers, which they framed and added to the walls of party rooms. Easy to maintain rattan furniture was perfect for these settings. In Hawai'i, it found its way into the homes of people at every level of society.

The design of rattan furniture was considered at the time to be "modern" in appearance. Its streamlined, smooth look extended to other types of design for the home, such as the softening of cor-ners in radios and kitchen appliances. Even automobiles featured that smooth swooping look. In Honolulu it was sold at retailer C.S. Wo as "fashion flow" furniture. But perhaps the leader in rattan was the Rattan Art Gallery, with its guiding force William Penn Aiton. Aiton made sure he was current with the design tastes of the time and opened a very modern building on Kalākaua Avenue in Waikīkī. He had the rattan components made in the Philippines, and then the final assembly was done in Hawai'i.

The period of the late 1930s through the 1950s saw an entire tropical romantic ambiance evolve—some of it good, but much of it kitschy. The complete look included koa and monkey pod furniture and accessories, split-bamboo drapery, Don Blanding prints and dishes, and ceramic male and female hula figures. On lānai and interior floors, which were often stained cement scored into grid patterns or wood, people placed sea-grass squares or lauhala mats.

Rattan enjoyed a revival in the 1980s and 1990s, though much of the new furniture simply copied older designs. The original pieces have become popular collectors' items in both Hawai'i and on the West Coast.

Opposite top: A brick floor and rough-hewn posts surrounded by lush foliage at the Honolulu home of Mr. and Mrs. Theodore A. Cooke, circa 1934.

Opposite bottom: A pool pavilion and party house was designed by renowned architect Vladimir Ossipoff to take advantage of the outdoors. Interior designer Jonathan Staub has freshened the space, while keeping the old rattan and bark-cloth vintage feel.

Left: The lānai of the Kaua'i home of Mr. and Mrs. G. P. Wilcox, circa 1937.

Below: A recent update keeps this lānai looking fresh, with upholstery inspired by old bark-cloth designs, a stone floor, and vintage 1950s chairs by Danish modernist Hans Wegner. The rattan pieces were a design collaboration between Mary Philpotts and Miller Fong. Philpotts designed furniture with Fong's father, Danny Ho Fong, early in her career, and the pieces remain in the company line.

Right: Danish teak chairs from the 1950s still look "right" on this lānai.

Opposite: The rich, warmth of blond rattan is as popular today as it was in its heyday in the 1940s and 1950s.

Right: Mid-century Hawaiian style reigns in this view of a suite at the Royal Hawaiian Hotel on Waikīkī Beach. Note the use again of lauhala mats and rattan furniture.

Below left: An elaborate rattan pūne'e, circa 1934, allows for the display of books and other items, as well as lounging.

Below right: Close-up of the kind of vintage floral upholstery prints popular during the 1930s, '40s, and '50s from the collection of Claudia Hurfert.

Opposite: A lounge at the Moloka'i Ranch Lodge, by architect Philip White and designer Mary Philpotts, is a seamless transition from the nostalgic mid-century to today.

THE PŪNE‘E

If one piece of furniture in the Hawaiian home can be called "beloved," it would be the pūne‘e. This moveable couch or bed is seen everywhere—in corners of living rooms, on lānai, doubling as a guest bed in an extra room, even in kitchens.

The pūne‘e began as a hikie‘e, a large stack of lauhala mats used by Native Hawaiians for sleeping and lounging in grass houses. When the first Western furniture began showing up in Hawai‘i, Hawaiians were fascinated with four-poster beds, which many acquired and placed in their grass homes as status symbols. Although the bed took up much of the space, Hawaiians rarely slept in them, preferring their traditional mats.

There is an illustration, done in 1837 by a British artist, that shows a meeting between Kamehameha III and several ships' officers. The officers are all sitting on Western chairs, and the Hawaiians are facing them, lounging on an enormous hikie‘e.

The huge hikie‘e often accommodated an entire family and were placed in the center of the room. Some were set on platforms to keep them off the ground. When Westerners adopted the hikie‘e, they scaled down the size, making it more easily moveable. This was the birth of the pūne‘e, as the smaller bed was called.

The pūne‘e today is used for everything from a sofa substitute on a lānai or porch, to a place to take an afternoon nap or watch television. In the middle of the 20th century pūne‘e were created from single or double beds, with lots of pillows or bolsters added for comfort and support. Some were custom-made frames made of native woods, or even rattan. "Pūne‘e naps" usually meant that the person would be sleeping beneath a kīhei pili, or lightweight cotton covering.

Today, with the trend toward Indonesian furniture for a rustic, tropical look, the pūne‘e can be seen as teak platforms with four legs and sometimes intricate carving. Whatever its form, the much loved pūne‘e is a mainstay in Hawaiian interior design.

This large renovated kitchen in an old Nu‘uanu home has carefully included a comfortable pūne‘e for friends and family, traditional stained board-and-batten walls, old koa furniture, and ‘ōhi‘a flooring for a look that will never become dated. The chair originally belonged to Judge Hermann Widemann, nicknamed "Oo" (as in "Lou"); it was known as his "thinking chair." The back adjusts to two positions.

"Hoa kīhei pili" is a naughty Hawaiian saying that means, literally, a *"coverlet companion"*—someone with whom one is having an affair. *Kīhei pili* are coverings used while napping on *pūneʻe.*

Excerpted from *Oʻlelo Noʻeau.*

Opposite: Designer Jonathan Staub updated this pūneʻe with new bark-cloth cushions. The old rattan chairs, along with walls washed to resemble driftwood, give this pool house a timeless Island quality.

Above: The geometric forms of this 1930s pūneʻe are influenced by classic Chinese design. The Japanese folding screen, lauhala mat, and rattan chairs evoke the melting-pot aspect of many Hawaiian rooms.

Below: A contemporary koa pūneʻe made by Martin & MacArthur has turned legs, which give it an old-fashioned look. The Japanese sliding windows are typical of mid-century houses designed by architect Vladimir Ossipoff.

Opposite: Custom upholstery fabrics being silkscreened by Hawaiian Hand Prints for use in Island homes, circa 1949.

Center: A piece of vintage leaf-print bark cloth was rescued by Mary Philpotts from the floor of the old Commercial Club in Honolulu before Group 70 occupied the space on the corner of King and Bethel streets.

Above: Dramatic tropical leaf-patterned curtains cascade to the floor in this circa 1934 home belonging to the Fagan family on O'ahu. Fabrics such as this were popular in many sunny climates at this time and suited the Islands particularly well.

Top: The lounge area of this beach pavilion at the Kaupoa cabins on Moloka'i Ranch strikes a nostalgic note, with board-and-batten construction, old carved mahogany furniture, and bark-cloth upholstery. Even the rods and reels are reminiscent of the 1950s. The architect is Philip White, and interior design is by Mary Philpotts.

Below: Hand-screened fabrics from Hawaiian Hand Prints are shown in this photograph taken in a showroom at Rattan Art Gallery in 1949.

Opposite: A vintage feel is accomplished by using an old water pitcher, glasses, and tablecloth on outdoor furniture designed by Walter Lamb using copper tubing. Similar furniture was later manufactured by Brown Jordan.

Above: The pūne'e and barrel chair by designer Walter Lamb are mainstays on this old Island lānai.

Right: The 1930s music cabinet, now used to conceal a television, is made of pale Philippine mahogany and attributed to designer Walter Lamb. The nostalgic hula doll collectibles on top reflect the owner's sense of humor. The two floral paintings on the wall are by Frank Oda. Interior design is by Mary Philpotts.

Opposite top: A poolside lounge chair by Walter Lamb, with lighthearted flamingo sculptures.

Opposite below: Walter Lamb's chair, originally made of copper tubing and laced rope, mixes easily with the rattan furniture, Asian screen, and brick floor of this circa 1940 lānai at the old Harrison home on Wailupe Circle.

Left: The lack of boundaries between inside and out is illustrated in this contemporary home by Honolulu architect David Stringer. There is a clean, open, linear quality to the spaces. In the foreground is an outdoor dining group from Brown Jordan in the style of earlier Walter Lamb furniture. The interiors were done by Mary Philpotts.

Above: Designer Walter Lamb's outdoor furniture is ideal for pool- or ocean-side lounging. It is shown here at the old Bright and Bradley homes in Honolulu.

Pewter and bronze and hammered brass

Old carved wood and gleaming glass,

Candles in polychrome candlesticks

And peasant lamps in floating wicks,

Dragons in silk on a Mandarin suite

In a chest that is filled with vagabond loot,

All of the beautiful useless things

That a vagabond's aimless drifting brings.

From *Vagabond's House* by Don Blanding

INFLUENCES

During the first half of the 20th century, immigrants to the Islands exerted a potent influence on Hawaiian interior design. Haole families, sometimes intermarried with Hawaiians, created spaces that incorporated items from both cultures. A nod to European elegance was combined with prized Hawaiian woods and artifacts. As the Chinese and Japanese gained strength and status, they, too, added to the eclectic mix with distinctively Asian forms. Beach, ranch, and plantation houses had a rough and ready look all their own. It was all an essentially Hawaiian mix.

EUROPEAN TRADITIONAL

Beginning in the 19th century, the best Western-style Hawaiian homes were a potpourri, a blending of old Hawaiian artifacts, calabashes, stone poi pounders, poi boards, plush Victorian sideboards, and ornately carved Chinese chairs and daybeds. In Hawaiian, kama'āina means "native born," or a "child of the land." Another use of the term is as a way to describe Hawai'i's old and frequently affluent families, those whose heritage dates to the days of early Western contact. Some of these family homes still survive. Their style casually mixes precious and humble, old and new items from many cultures, along with a relaxed naturalness. A kama'āina is one whose roots in Hawai'i are solid—merely spending time in the Islands is not enough. With the term comes a host of subtle meanings that explain behavior and attitudes considered typically "Island." Being kama'āina implies a connection of the soul to the land.

Right: The chest and chair are original to the house. The old wicker floral stand belonged to the owner's grandmother. The photographs of ladies on the wall are all relatives of the owner.

Below: The living room at "Lihiwai," the Honolulu home of Mrs. George Carter.

Right: The dining room of this Honolulu residence, with its blend of traditional European forms, reflects the style of the original owners in 1920. The oil portrait is of the owner's mother as a child. The home is by architect Hart Wood for the Van Poole family.

Below: In this photo of the Monnett home in Honolulu, taken in the early 20th century, we see a similar room filled with portraits, Victorian, French, and Spanish furniture, and a heavily beamed ceiling. The timber beams were articulated differently from room to room, depending on the mood the architect wanted to create.

Opposite: The similarities between the circa 1934 photo of the living room in the Fagan home and the modern day Nu'uanu home below are remarkable. Notice the same lauhala mats on the floor and the easy mix of Hawaiian and Western pieces.

Preceding page: The two chairs in front of the fireplace were in the home when the owner purchased it. A lush arrangement of anthurium and tropicals from the yard sit before colorful woodblock prints by Paul Jacoulet.

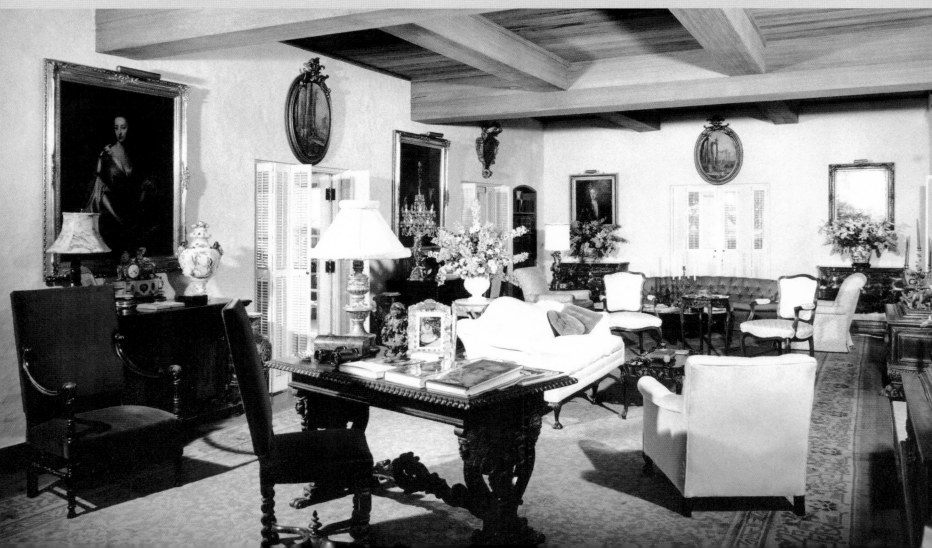

A lauhala mat placed on a pigmented concrete floor and paneled and pickled walls are both classic Island design elements that give this family room a timeless quality. The architect is Hart Wood, and the interior designer Mary Philpotts.

Author and historian Irving Jenkins spotted a collection of furniture being sold off in Honolulu and called the owner of this Nu'uanu home. The owner believed at first that it was the work of noted designer George Moody of Grossman-Moody, Ltd. It had been made expressly for the Pemperton family in the 1930s. The furniture is now thought to have been designed by Walter Lamb after similar pieces attributed to him were found in old museum photos.

The grouping included a dining table which could be extended and chairs of Philippine mahogany. The chairs had seats made of rattan peel which were woven over the frames. The pieces became the centerpiece and unifying factor in the room. The torchères inspired by the ti plants are believed to be from Gump's.

Two card tables from Gump's came from the late Ernie Kai and now face each other on both sides of the room. The old koa chairs were acquired over time. The large poi board is from the 19th century and was a gift. It was found standing straight up on the beach after a storm and is believed to be among the largest ever found. The owner had a stand made for it in the shape of a Polynesian head rest, and it now serves as a coffee table.

Above: The library at Roseland, the Nu'uanu home of Mrs. Alfred Castle.

Below: This round center table, made primarily of koa and inlaid with various Hawaiian woods, belonged to the owner's grandparents. It was most likely made in the late 19th century.

Opposite: The large koa dining table was made in Hilo in the 1960s. An early oil painting of a Hawaiian woman wearing a cowboy hat is by artist Pegge Hopper. The kamani and koa sideboard is a family heirloom; a similar piece is on display at Hulihe'e Palace in Kailua-Kona. The delicately plaited lauhala mat is from Tahiti, and the old hand-painted European chairs belonged to the owner's mother.

Opposite: The koa bed and dresser shown here have been together as far back as the owner can remember. The headboard is decorated with milo wood accents. The original bird illustrations are by Volcano artist Marian Berger.

Above: The contemporary chaise was designed by Jon Martin of Martin & MacArthur. It is hand-made of koa with a cane center.

Left: An ancient Hawaiian stone poi pounder doubles as a doorstop in this kama'āina Big Island home.

Preceding pages: The rich layering of koa walls with koa furnishings deepens the earthy feel of these Big Island rooms.

Above: The four-poster bed made by artisan-craftsman McD Philpotts of Big Island koa wood has been turned in the style of the late 1800s. The bench is Indonesian, and the painted screen is by Robert Lee Eskridge.

Right: An antique koa cabinet holds calabashes used by Native Hawaiians for storage and food. On the wall behind is a koa wood plaque of mangoes carved in relief by Franz Otremba.

Opposite: Beside the koa four-poster bed is an old chest of drawers transformed with hand-painted wood inlay and a traditional Island maile lei by Georg James and John Dinsmore. The artists are known for turning rescued furniture into beautiful and nostalgic pieces of art.

Left: The handcrafted table and chairs and silk-screened fabric, shown in the Fagan home in 1934, reflect the rich Island craft culture that existed in the mid-1900s.

Below left: The contemporary console was designed by Mary Philpotts and Dominique Fraikin. It features a hand-cut top of Big Island basalt. The koa casework is by Martin & MacArthur.

Below: A large batik painting of traditionally attired Hawaiians by artist Yvonne Cheng dominates this corner of a Big Island beach house. Below sits a bench by Henry Dimond, an early missionary furniture maker in the 19th century. It once belonged to the owner's grandmother.

Coconut containers on either end of the bench were inherited from the owner's grandparents and are believed to be from the South Seas. A Chinese altar table divides the room. Interior design by Mary Philpotts.

Above: The koa four-poster in the style of the 19th century was recently made by Big Island craftsman Bob Shepherd. A hand-sewn traditional Hawaiian quilt in a ginger lei pattern tops it, giving a vintage feel to a modern bedroom. Hawaiian women were taught the art of quilting by missionary wives in the early 1800s. They soon developed their own unique style, using motifs from nature. A handmade quilt such as this can take as long as a year to complete.

Right: The ornate Victorian "what not" is a family heirloom believed to have been brought by the owner's grandparents from Japan. It sits in contrast to the otherwise contemporary pieces in the home.

HAWAIIAN REBORN

The best in Hawaiian design refers back to the ancient Hawaiian value system—a profound love of the land, or the ʻāina, and love of family and ancestors, their legacies and artifacts. Even in the fast-paced world of modern Hawaiʻi, these values hold true, making Islanders less likely to be slaves to fashion and catalog shopping than most places on the mainland.

Hawaiians have a propensity to move more slowly, to build rooms piece by piece, and to hang on to the results once they are achieved. In other parts of the country, individualism in interior design is becoming more popular. In Hawaiʻi it has always been the case. Perhaps this began because goods took so long to arrive by ship, or maybe the differences in attitude were driven by the particular dictates of the climate.

Whatever the explanation, the important idea is that when you get it right, you create lasting value, a look that will endure through all the latest trends. Call it "getting the bones right." The most successful rooms always reflect the people who inhabit them.

Above: A low antique Chinese sideboard, with calabashes to one side, greets you at the entrance to this new Honolulu home.

Below: Marquesan tattoos inspired the patterns of this coffee table and the library table on the opposite page. The sketch is by Georg James. The tables were designed by James, John Dinsmore and McD Philpotts. They were custom-made by artisan McD Philpotts.

Opposite: The living room of this Honolulu home, designed by architect Philip "Pip" White, is kept cool by fans and a high ceiling covered in grass matting. The triptych, done in oil, of Island women in a hala grove is by Arthur Johnsen. The room doubles as a library and music room. Interior design is by Mary Philpotts and Belinda Akaka.

Right: The koa sofa table was made for the home by Martin & MacArthur. Glass insets made to resemble water in a stream were created by Bill Grix Art.

Below right: A closeup of the Polynesian tattoo design on the handmade koa table by McD Philpotts.

Opposite: Two acrylic-on-linen triptychs were created for two sides of the living room by Island artist Arthur Johnsen.

*Ho'i ka 'o'opu 'ai lehua
i ka mapunapuna.*

Going back to the source.
(Hawaiian Proverb)

Opposite: The dining room table, inspired by one at the old Walker Estate on Pali Highway, was made by Martin & MacArthur. The absence of window coverings when not needed is typical of Island homes. The windows are custom designed and the floors made of 'ōhi'a wood.

Top: This detail of the dining table shows a curly koa veneer inset with a kapa-patterned inlay border. The edges are finished in koa. The look of wood-on-wood creates a richness that is complemented by nature.

Left: Koa rockers being glued and clamped in a workshop at Martin & MacArthur's Honolulu factory.

Opposite: Lying on the bed, the owner is able to take in the lush beauty of his garden. A cozy corner for reading is set up with a generous, comfortable wicker chair, and a wooden Chinese hat box is used as an end table.

Top: Architect Philip "Pip" White added a board-and-batten wall behind the master bed as a reference to old-time Island exterior architecture connecting the outside to the inside. The Hawaiian quilt gives the room a cozy traditional Hawaiian ambiance.

Above: The koa dresser by Martin & MacArthur was further adorned with painted ferns picked from the owner's garden. The painted reverse pochoir technique on the fern motif was done by Georg James.

Following pages: The outdoor shower surrounded by foliage was created by landscape consultants Lois Nottage, Jean Thomas, and Leland Miyano. The copper pipe is wrapped around a faux tree trunk.

HAWAIIAN VALLEY BUNGALOW

Bungalows by their very nature are cozy. They lack a certain seriousness and grandness. Island bungalows are no different, whether built on a beach on the North Shore or as a rambling cottage in Honolulu. The hallmark of a bungalow is its manageability and modest, easy atmosphere. You will often find a porch or sunroom and an open floor plan.

This bungalow, built in the 1920s, has been renovated to accommodate modern living. Awnings were added to the exterior, which originally had no eaves for shelter from rain and sun. Small bedrooms in the original house have become an office, library, and dining room. The owners had Island architect Geoffrey Lewis add a large master suite and bath, almost doubling the size of the home. Still, it retains its essential cottage-like nature. It reflects the owners' Island heritage, now enhanced with Asian elements.

Above: Awnings provide shade to this 1920s valley bungalow. The landscaping, by Lois Nottage and Jean Thomas, includes old-fashioned ti plants and lauae ferns, as well as kukui trees.

Opposite: The entrance includes an old handmade koa table inherited by the owners, an oversized Indonesian teak chair, and lauhala mat. Designer Marion Philpotts Miller worked with the owners to pull old and new pieces into a pleasing mix.

Following pages: The open floor plan in which the entry flows gracefully into the living area is typically Island in style.

Opposite: This addition to a 1920s Nu'uanu valley cottage includes a vaulted ceiling and stained-cement floor. Chinese doors were added for privacy from a sitting room, and near the shuttered window sits an antique koa bench by 19th-century cabinetmaker Henry Weeks. The architect is Geoffrey Lewis.

Above: The ethnic feeling of the sitting room is enhanced by an Indonesian ikat draped over a bright blue ceramic jar, and by a collection of batik-covered pillows on the sofa. The oil painting of Honolulu's Chinatown is by artist Pamela Andelin.

Below: The owners took apart a folding Thai screen and had it reassembled in a frame to allow air flow and give privacy from neighbors. An Indonesian textile hanger displays Javanese batiks. The area is perfect for warm-weather dining.

Classical Cottage Looks to the East

This two-story 1920s cottage was so termite-eaten it had to be almost completely rebuilt. Designer Marion Philpotts Miller gave new life to the home by preserving the original structure, with its symmetrical columns and deep lānai, and painting the columns a modern black, uncovering the original pigmented cement floor, and adding a lap pool for drama in the sliver of front yard that remained.

All the floors were replaced with rich hardwood and the walls painted in several shades of white and cream to add depth and interest. The bedrooms, baths, and closets were reconfigured and outfitted in a stripped-down contemporary way—with new simple, clean finishes. Asian chairs and art objects mix easily with Island family heirlooms, carefully edited for a minimal, youthful look.

It's now a family home filled with noisy barefoot kids, sleeping dogs, and music in every room.

This page: The fresh minimal style of interior designer Marion Philpotts Miller is seen in this bright, unfussy home for a young family. The lack of window coverings allows maximum light to enter the room. The color scheme is kept subdued, with white couches and black-and-white mud-cloth cushions. The accents are contemporary and Asian inspired.

Opposite: An orchid in a calabash of Hawaiian wood, black Asian panels, tabletop items, and bare floors all provide a seamless flow between rooms. Fresh leaves from the owners' garden give a sense of the lushness outside.

Previous page: Teak Indonesian lounge chairs are constantly rearranged to suit the occasion. Note the pūneʻe at the end of the lānai positioned for an afternoon nap.

Opposite: The sleek lines of the chairs and window seat contrast with the old koa table and simple country Chinese chair. Japanese tables are stacked and topped with fresh anthuriums and ginger from a local floral shop.

Top left: The family pets have their own little corner of the kitchen.

Bottom left: Interior designer Marion Philpotts Miller created this contemporary kitchen by combining several smaller rooms into a single large one and adding clean-lined surfaces and appliances. The hardwood floors are as practical as they are beautiful.

Above: The built-in pūne'e in the kitchen allows the children to visit while meals are being prepared. Built-in storage below is always welcome.

He hale kanaka, ke 'alala ala
No keiki, ke hae ala no ka 'ilio.

It is an inhabited house where the sounds of children and the bark of a dog are heard. (Hawaiian proverb)

THE BEACH BUNGALOW IS LIGHT AND SASSY

The best beach houses lack pretense. Built for family and friends to relax and read, to nap in the afternoon, and to watch children play in the surf, they have become rarer in the Islands as beach real estate prices soar. But once upon a time, it was common for families to keep beach houses for weekend and summer use on the hot, dry leeward coasts of all the Islands.

The interior is kept neutral and fresh with white paint and new finishes. There is no precious art here—just bleached white coral, old bottles, and glass balls found on the beach. Canoe paddles become wall art, and washable fabrics are meant for lounging with sandy feet.

The key to designing a beach bungalow is to avoid anything that cannot take hard wear. With our year-round summer, Hawaiian beach houses get lots of use. Nothing kills relaxation as quickly as having to worry about expensive, high-maintenance furnishings.

Preceding pages: There is a timeless quality about this renovated Windward O'ahu beach cottage, restored as a weekend retreat for several generations of an Island family. The love of outdoor dining, the need for shelter from the sun, and the lack of pretense make its design ideal. Board-and-batten siding is a typical feature of many old Island cottages.

Left: The shaded stone path leading to the cottage gives relief from the sun.

Below: The organization of this small children's room allows for multiple sleeping and play options. Ease of use and materials that can handle the elements are most important in planning a beach house. The spaces were designed by Jonathan Staub and Marion Philpotts Miller.

Following pages: The nautical blues and whites on ample sofas encourage relaxation. Old bottles, shells, coral and Japanese glass balls make an impromptu arrangement.

Hawaiian Ranch and Plantation

It would make most inhabitants of Hawai'i's ranch and plantation homes laugh to hear that their houses are thought to have a certain interior "style" or "design." They have always been meant as utilitarian shelter. Living on ranches and plantations meant working long hours, going to bed early, and rising before the sun.

This style, shown here at Moloka'i Ranch, arises from a tough work environment. There are rougher finishes and more washable materials than places in town. Verandas often wrap around the sides of post-and-railing houses stained green or brick-red. Worn saddles thrown on railings become "art," and the dining table can be as prosaic as a picnic table placed in a kitchen.

Ranch and plantation style is comfortable and casual. These are rooms meant to nurture people who work hard and play hard. So they can put their feet up, chairs have ottomans. Lauhala and other straw hats hang on pegs or a hat stand by the door. Off-hours are filled with the care and feeding of animals—be they hunting dogs, goats, or chickens. When ranch and plantation people acquire material goods, they tend to be precious feather lei for hats, or quilts for the beds. The walls are laden with photographs of family and friends in mismatched frames—collections that grow organically and mysteriously over a period of years. Scrapbooks lie on tables, memories of summers and rodeos past. Moloka'i Ranch, now a resort, has worked to maintain the legacy of a working ranch. The main lodge is a virtual museum of nostalgia.

Top: The Moloka'i Ranch Lodge sits on top of a hill on Moloka'i's west end. The new lodge was designed by architect Philip "Pip" White and is located in the plantation town of Maunaloa.

Opposite: Interior designer Mary Philpotts instructed artists Georg James and John Dinsmore to "pack up their paints and go to Moloka'i." There they decorated every surface they felt needed it, from mirrors to naked elevator walls, and even this old Japanese tansu with a nostalgic hula girl.

Opposite: The great room of Moloka'i Ranch Lodge has tough leather sofas and vintage rattan, sold to the owners by the late collector Robert Van Dyke. The old rattan was covered in vintage bark cloth gathered from collections across the mainland and Hawai'i.

Above: The wooden table, studded mirror, and pots all have a rough-hewn ranch look. The boots actually belonged to cowboys who came to the lodge shortly before it opened. They left their boots at the request of the designer, who then had them nailed to the floor to provide authentic atmosphere.

Left: The casual seating area is made up of more vintage rattan from the Van Dyke collection.

This cozy corner of the Moloka'i Ranch Lodge could just as easily have been photographed fifty years ago. Moloka'i Ranch has developed a resort on the west end of the Island that takes into consideration the rural and historic nature of the area.

Moloka'i has always been a no-nonsense, rough-and-tumble kind of place. The resort blends into the landscape, with low-impact structures such as this lodge, a nod to the area's rural past, and a series of "tentalows" on the beach at Kaupoa.

The furniture for this nook was acquired by interior designer Mary Philpotts from collector Robert Van Dyke.

ASIAN INFLUENCE

Hawai'i is, after all, halfway to Asia. The influx of Chinese and Japanese workers to Hawaiian sugar and pineapple plantations in the late 19th century brought an Asian sensibility to the Islands. At first, workers' homes did not reflect the finer attributes of their homelands, but as people left the plantations and became successful in business and the professions, they looked East for inspiration. The growing awareness of a distinctly Hawaiian interior design in the early decades of the 20th century blossomed into a strong movement by 1930. Not only did Island architects build to suit the climate and culture, but designers emerged to furnish these spaces with an Island sensibility.

Designer Alice Spalding Bowen convinced the prestigious Gump's store in San Francisco to open a branch in Honolulu. Gump's was already well-established, with a fine reputation for Asian antiques and home furnishings. In 1929, they opened a groundbreaking and influential store at the corner of Kalākaua and Lewers Road in Waikīkī. Bowen became their first manager.

George H. Moody was made Gump's first Island designer. It didn't take Gump's long to discover that they would need to produce items especially for the Island market. Hawai'i was still quite removed from the mainland, and Island lifestyles reflected this. Moody began by designing furniture with clean lines, using traditional Island motifs. Hawaiian women wove lauhala mats to stretch over frames for streamlined dining chairs; koa, monkey pod, and mahogany were bleached a light yellow; and furniture, much of it carved with plant and flower patterns, was built. Island artists such as Isami Doi were also commissioned to add designs to the store's merchandise.

Moody employed his talents in jewelry designs for earrings, pins, and bracelets in gold, silver, and ivory. For a time, he also designed jewelry for H. F. Wichman and Company, a local jeweler. In 1936,

Moody left to form his own company with his partner, Edward S. Grossman. The two opened Grossman-Moody, Ltd. in downtown Honolulu at King and Alakea streets, where Moody continued to design and sell furniture, jewelry, table and house wares. In the 1950s the company moved to a store on Kalākaua Avenue in Waikīkī.

World War II saw a huge influx of military personnel to Hawai'i. In spite of the war, or perhaps because of it, a great deal of entertaining and partying went on in Honolulu, and even on the Neighbor Islands. A need developed for gifts that could be taken home to the mainland. During this period, small items for the home, as well as tropically inspired jewelry of a much lower quality, were mass-produced.

The end of the war signaled a desire for a changed, modern world. Housing for young families was needed, and the focus in home design switched from items produced for a privileged elite to those that met the needs of the general populace. Gump's closed their Waikīkī store in 1951. The talented Moody retired in 1969.

Right: An Asian-inspired garden structure at Mokumoa, the home of Mrs. Frank Damon, circa 1930s. Drawing by Georg James.

Opposite top: The trim on the Spalding home on Makiki Heights was Asian influenced. This beautiful home is now The Contemporary Museum. The pool is no longer there, and the museum café is located downstairs.

Opposite below: The interior of the Albert F. Afong residence in Nu'uanu Valley called "Laimi," meaning "awaiting the day." The house was built near the site where Kamehameha I rested his army the night before the battle that helped unite the Islands under one rule.

JAPANESE STYLE ALLOWS COOLING TRADEWINDS

When Vladimir Ossipoff designed this hill-top sanctuary in 1956 he did his best to take advantage of the gentle tradewinds while giving shelter from the hot, Hawaiian sun. His care has made living in the house a pleasure over the years. It has also turned the life inside the house toward outdoors instead of having to encase the owners in sealed-in air-conditioning. In the late 1990s the house was renovated by Ossipoff's longtime partner, Sidney Snyder. They added a bedroom wing, new dining room, and adjoining kitchen, but left the original house basically the same.

Interior designers Mary Philpotts and Marion Philpotts Miller both assisted the owner in Hawai'i and in San Francisco. Oceans apart, they created a synergy. At Gump's in San Francisco the owner fell in love with an old Japanese screen from the Kamakura period depicting the Heiji Rebellion for the living room. Another view of the living room is framed by a window which casts a warm glow on the adjoining dining terrace.

Top: The Chinese motifs on the dining chairs have a simplicity of design that combines with beautiful Asian screens to give the Monnett home on Mākālei Place a spare elegance. Circa 1934.

Below: The same combination of a large screen and furniture with dramatic Asian detail give the Hayward home at Black Point a timeless quality. Photographed in 1934.

Opposite: The glamour of this Honolulu dining room is punctuated by the Chinese altar table and screen at the far end of the room. The table has a formal European look, and together with the Chippendale chairs and Persian carpet gives the whole room an Old World richness. The Chinese screen shows the Eight Immortals and the deity of longevity.

Following pages: The house with its Japanese overtones glows like a lantern at night.

A Japanese Teahouse Looks West

When the owners moved into this mid-century Honolulu home it was so perfect they did very little aside from softening the redwood ceiling and beams with a grey wash. Architect Vladimir Ossipoff, a master of the art of building for the site, had designed it near a private golf course back in 1956.

It's always fortunate to inherit pieces from relatives with good taste, and in this case the couple lucked out. The husband's parents had been in Japan in the 1950s and purchased beautiful screens, tansus, and Imari ceramics. They also inherited his mother's two six-foot

long sofas upholstered in a dynamic blue-and-white pattern which added an interesting contrast.

The home owes a spiritual similarity to many of the rooms designed by Robert Ansteth shown opposite right. Ansteth was passionate about horizontal, linear design which he created for the best Honolulu homes in the 1950s, '60s and '70s. Many of Ansteth's pieces were made especially for his clients, and he regularly turned interesting Asian objects into lamps, end tables, and wall art. The home's refurbishment was by Joan Moynahan.

Opposite, above and left: Strong, Japanese screens, low linear furniture, and tansus used as end tables, hall trunks and even coffee tables are part of the signature Robert Ansteth look which gained popularity in the mid-century and remains timeless to this day.

Top: The contemporary Kāhala home has the same no-fuss attitude that it did in when it was built in 1959. Chrome chairs and shoji screens give the interiors a modern look while nodding to an earlier era.

Above: A bedroom opens directly onto a private inner courtyard, giving the entire home a Zen-like quality. Interior design and refurbishment by Judie and Richard Malmgrem and Kathy Merrill.

Opposite: Stones, stones everywhere. The inner courtyard and sliding doors that lead in to living spaces give this home the feeling of being in Japan. The architecture allows for the ultimate in outdoor living.

The beams of my house will be fragrant wood

that once in a teeming jungle stood . . .

The roof must have a rakish dip

To shadowy eaves where the rain can drip

In a damp, persistent tuneful way

It's a cheerful sound on a gloomy day.

From *Vagabond's House* by Don Blanding

MID-CENTURY EVOLUTION

Initially, cultural design references were applied to the outsides of buildings in the form

of trims, windows, and doors. But by the middle of the 20th century, architects trained in

the Beaux Arts tradition had developed a more international style. Vladimir Ossipoff, Bert

Ives, Tommy Perkins, and others reinvented Asian forms, using them in the actual design

of the spaces. Interiors followed their lead. The result was a crisp modernity.

The '50s and '60s

In the 1950s a new group of architects and designers introduced a decisive modernity to Hawaiian design. They believed, quite simply, that "less is more."

Among those who preferred uncluttered purity were architects Vladimir Ossipoff, Sid Snyder, Tommy Perkins, Bert Ives, George Hogan, Pete Wimberly, Harry Bent, Don Chapman, Frank Haines, Richard Tongg, Alfred Preis, and designers Robert Ansteth, Alice Spalding Bowen, and Phyllis Spalding.

Ansteth became well known for his linear Japanese-inspired rooms filled with artifacts and items from the Orient made into lamps, tables, and decorative pieces. Large, exquisite Japanese and Chinese screens almost always graced the walls.

Lamb's furniture designs for the Island market are now especially treasured period pieces. Among them are the clean-lined and sturdy outdoor tables and chairs he made from salvaged copper tubing and strong, interlaced rope. His pieces are treasured heritage items although only a couple of decades old, perhaps because the forms fit design minimalism so well.

Hawai'i architects of the mid-century created spaces that dissolved the walls between the inside and the outside. They did this through the use of large glass doors and windows that, in most cases, slid open and shut as the weather dictated. Stone was left in its natural state. Wood was stained to a silvery finish to resemble driftwood, and copper weathered to a lovely green-blue patina. Bronze was left unpolished.

Ventilation, and the positioning of the house on the lot to attract the cooling breezes, took on the utmost importance. Fancy finishes and moldings were scrapped in favor of austere, clean lines. The look was modern and international, while at the same time it suited the Island lifestyle.

In 1958, *House Beautiful* magazine dedicated an entire issue to Hawaiian interior design. They described the postwar period as "never crude or ostentatious." There was a serenity and courteous quality to dwellings. They were composed and private, dignified but informal. Walls and fences went to the property lines, and the division between the indoors and out faded. Everywhere, the love of craftsmanship and blended cultural furnishings was seen.

Right: Hawaiian and Asian elements mix effortlessly. A Balinese ceramic wedding couple and orchids in a monkeypod bowl sit on top of a custom-made flea market find coffee table. The koa rocker is from Martin & MacArthur.

Opposite: This mid-century house on Maunalani Heights was designed by Ossipoff, Snyder & Rowland. The sliding Japanese doors open all the rooms out onto a central courtyard. The hall floors are polished black pigmented cement.

Top: An old koa tree dominates the bricked central court filled with Asian pots and a comfortable outdoor dining area.

Left: The floor-to-ceiling windows, natural wood wall treatment, and rattan bucket chairs in this vintage Kāhala Avenue home are timeless elements in Island design.

Above left: Architect Sid Snyder designed this Nu'uanu Valley home with pale rubbed walls, open beams, and lots of special built-in features.

Above center: A vintage painting by regional master D. Howard Hitchcock hangs above a Japanese kiri wood tansu.

Above right: A typically Island arrangement of ti leaves and purple agapanthus sits on the table-top. On the wall is a skeletal scientific model that is 19th-century French.

Below: The Eastlake wing chair of curly maple is a favorite. The owner has photographs of both his father and his grandfather taken in the same chair. The painting is by Charles Schultz.

Opposite: The crimson boomerang sofa is vintage 1930s, and the abstract above the fireplace is a 1960s contemporary Japanese landscape. The fireplace gives the whole room a lift. The designer took it to an automotive shop and had it painted a high-gloss 1967 Mercedes green. Interior design by Jonathan Staub.

A Home Without Walls

Floor to ceiling screens span areas on two sides of this house, where normally there would be walls. As a result, sitting in the house makes one feel as if there are no boundaries to the outside and the view beyond. Built in 1940 by architect Allen Johnson of Johnson & Perkins, the simplicity of design and attention paid to the lay of the land has allowed the home to remain contemporary and serene in feeling, even as the city grew.

Interior designer Mary Philpotts helped the active, two-career couple living here select colors that are cool and quiet, and kept the lines of the furniture low and sleek, making this house a retreat from a hectic life. Remarkably, the screened "walls" allow the home to be filled with the scent of the plumeria blossoms outside.

Above: There is a quiet, timeless quality to this Allen Johnson house. He had a special ability to address the Hawaiian climate. Johnson preferred everything wide open "so you lived practically on the lānai."

Opposite top left: The home's airy dining area has the same feel as the '50s dining room at right.

Opposite top center: A Woodlawn Mānoa residence without barriers to the exterior by architect Richard Windisch, circa 1954.

Opposite top right: The dining room of a home at Diamond Head from about the same time.

Opposite below: The amazing green-stained ceiling has never been redone. Johnson claims he learned the detailing for his houses from local Japanese carpenters. The only barrier to the outside is the screen on this hallway leading to the master bedroom.

Right: Part of the owner's collection of Mexican and South American folk sculpture.

Below: African fertility figures sit on a Korean tansu. Above is an oil by artist Alan Leitner. The sculpture on the hallway wall is by Esther Shimazu. The painting on the red wall was done by Japanese modernist Genichero Inokuma, a friend of the owners.

SPLASHES OF FOLK ART AND COLOR

This art- and travel-loving couple have filled their Honolulu hilltop home with treasures from their travels. The pair have melded the colorful, naïve art of simple people the world over. The result is beautiful and harmonious.

Island architect John Hara designed the renovation for this 1970s home by adding more entertainment space and opening the house up to the spectacular city view.

The main living space soars; the room feels much larger than it is. Interesting collections of Mexican folk art, contemporary paintings by friends and acquaintances—and even some by the owner himself—cover every wall and surface. Korean chests mix with Portuguese and Spanish ceramics, Polynesian textiles, and Chinese dishes. The result is charming and elegant. Interior design by Mary Philpotts and Kristie Kiggins.

This page and opposite top: Architect David Stringer designs walls that seem to disappear; this linear quality is achieved by horizontal tracking of the woodwork. It was done so intricately with a laser beam level that there was a mere 1/16th of an inch of tolerance through the entire home. The house, on Wailupe Circle, flows seamlessly from street to oceanfront. Interior design by Mary Philpotts.

Opposite bottom left: Typical of mid-century interiors are strong clean lines and Asian accessories. Even the blinds are horizontal.

Opposite bottom right: Simple, horizontal lines and Asian accents at Florence Bates Hayward's Black Point home.

I've seen the shrines that men have made

Of porphyry with gold inlaid,

Marble, teak and carven jade.

Far more beautiful than all,

An ape blossom, slim and tall,

Curved in flawless ivory line,

Fashioning a flower-shrine

For beauty, goddess thrice-divine.

From "In an Old Hawaiian Garden" by Don Blanding

21ST-CENTURY HAWAIIAN

Island design has come to a geometric modernism, with its use of rich, tactile fabrics, classical South Pacific and Asian forms, and openness accented by the use of wood and stone. The best designs pay close attention to the ʻāina, or land, surrounding the home. Compatible cultures such as the Balinese and other Polynesian Islands are easily incorporated. We look to their graphic shapes in tattoos and kapa cloth. A reverence for natural surroundings is seen everywhere.

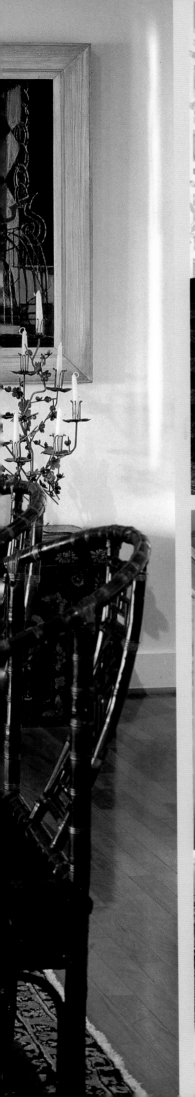

PERCHED ON A HILL

The owners of this hilltop jewel were delighted to find an older Honolulu home that already possessed a built-in sense of artistry. By adding their eclectic mix of antiques and contemporary art, some of which was created by the owner himself, they were able to give this gracious, open house warmth and a tropical richness. They did this by not being timid, by using diverse materials, and respecting what was already so good about the place. Large-scale, mellowed Asian antiques are everywhere, as are inherited items. Interior designer Mary Philpotts commissioned Georg James and John Dinsmore to create the mural of banana leaves on the wall.

In the evening, they sit on the lānai and watch the lights of Honolulu come on until their view sparkles.

BEACHCOMBERS AT DIAMOND HEAD

The San Francisco-based couple who spend months out of each year at this waterfront home near Waikīkī Beach brought a city sensibility and love of refined, clean lines to their second home. They'd purchased a basic white shell, but the location was unbeatable. The already good floor plan was personalized by designers Mary Philpotts and Barbara Rodrigues. One of the first things they did was to have respected Island furniture-makers, Martin & MacArthur, add teak millwork to the walls and finishes. They used Indonesian grills to redesign a television alcove as an unusual feature in the room. The result was a customized look and a light, tropical, Asian feeling.

Opposite top left: Rich embroidered moths adorn an ottoman.

Opposite top right: Three ceramic mandarins hold court on a hall side table.

Opposite below: Rich embroidered fabrics with an Asian sensibility are layered on twin beds in the guest room.

Below: Luxurious bedding and multiple silk embroidered pillows give this master bedroom a comfortable and inviting atmosphere. The designers continued the teak detailing into the recesses of existing drywall, creating definition to the bed and back walls. A ledge was added to hold decorative items. The interior design is by Mary Philpotts and Barbara Rodrigues.

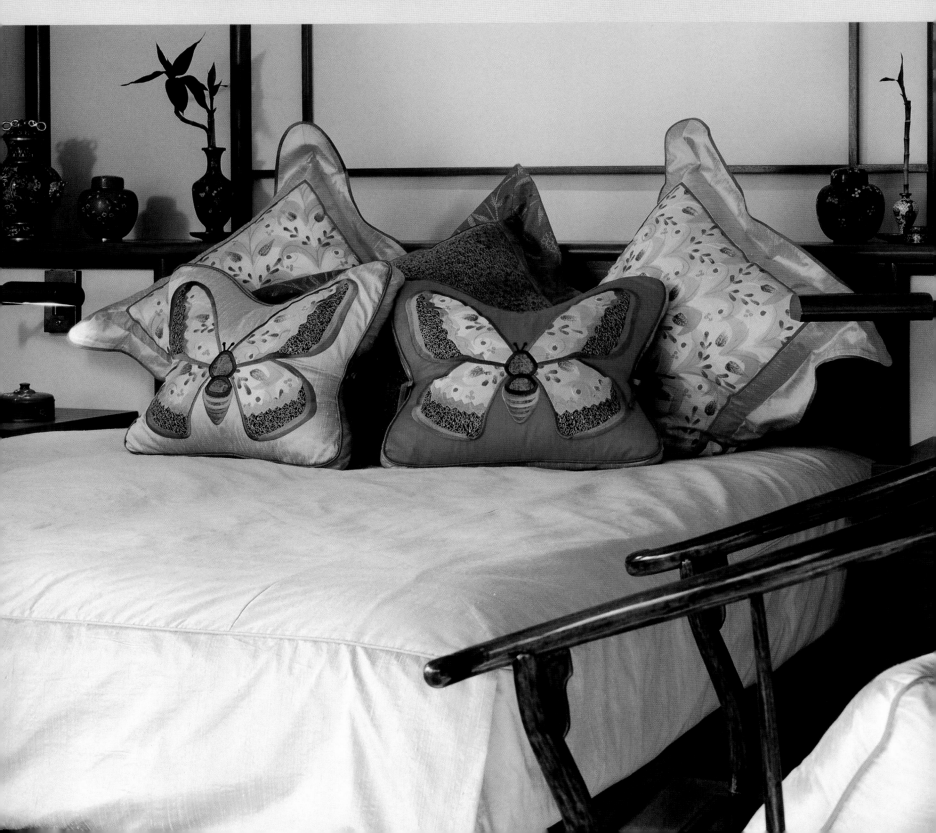

An Ode to Craftsmanship

So often a primary residence becomes an ever-growing mix of the ephemera of one's daily life. Starting again on a vacation dwelling, it's nice to be able to take one central idea and build the entire house around it. San Francisco architect Shay Zak wanted this Big Island home to celebrate its location. One of the key elements is the dropped windows close to the floor, which take advantage of all the views.

Interior designer Mary Philpotts worked with the owners to keep the furnishings harmonious and compatible to the ambiance of the home itself. Together they searched for and commissioned furnishings. Even the frames on the owner's collection of painter Avi Kiriaty's work were custom-made by local artisan Don Wilkenson. The dining table, with a foot ledge on the trestle base, was carefully crafted by Martin & MacArthur. Then the entire table was lightly scraped to give it a rippling finish by sunlight and candlelight.

HOUSE WITH VANISHING WALLS

When you build on the warm, leeward side of the Island, where early mornings and late evenings are the best times of the day, there is the urge to live without window coverings, heavy carpeting, and even walls. Singaporean architect Tan Hock Beng and American architect Kurt Mitchell have created a beachfront home with a seamless design intended to catch every cool breeze and be filled with light. The contemporary home is still textured, and Asian in feeling, with large-scale Balinese furnishings. Handcrafted one-of-a-kind objects are everywhere, and accessories add layering and warmth. Philpotts & Associates designer Lowell Tom used rich, warm colors with cooler accents for the upholstery and carpets. The result is an easy yet dramatic blend of both architecture and interior design.

Above: The architects and designer all agreed
this house should have vanishing walls that
allowed the outside in whenever possible. This
room, layered with Asian and handcrafted
pieces, celebrates this idea.

Right: Designer Lowell Tom kept the look of the
dining room contemporary by not using window
coverings and using natural, textured materials.
The Tibetan carpet in a floral pattern adds color.

Opposite: Interior designer Lowell Tom did not add drapery to this bedroom; he kept it open to celebrate the climate, the light, and the breezes. The massive four-poster bed faces the hala trees and the ocean beyond.

Above: Tom has kept the wood floors bare and used tropical patterns and lots of pillows to plump up the Indonesian carved platform bed. There is a solid, clean, and rich quality to every room of the house.

SLEEPING IN A GARDEN

One way to feel like you're living outdoors is to create a series of courtyards and surround them with pavilions where your life goes on. This private residence located on the Big Island has done that. The setting is everything, the interiors merely backdrops, albeit luxurious ones.

Disappearing pocket doors open both the lānai and living room to the balmy climate and afford views of the golf course, beach, and ocean that go on forever. In order to make the outside the most important feature, the interiors have been kept low-key, monochromatic, and earthy. This warm, natural palette is light and bright, with the liberal use of wood floors, cabinets, and built-ins, mats, rattan and woven furniture, and Hawaiian objects such as oversized kapa cloth and canoe paddles used as art.

Bedrooms have windows on three sides, with the bed placed in the middle of the room. Because much of the furniture is not anchored to walls, large neutral surfaces are exposed. The effect is of sleeping in a garden. Even the lavish glass showers look out on foliage. Interior design is by Mary Philpotts and Lowell Tom.

Architect Warren
Sunnland designed
this Big Island resi-
dence, where the
living spaces are
merely backdrops to
the lush exterior. This
four-poster is swathed
in luxurious silk
bedding, and the bed
is placed in the center
of the room to make
one feel as if sleeping
in the garden outside.
A large Polynesian
kapa cloth is framed
on one wall.

CONTEMPORARY BALINESE

The newcomer on the interior-design block in Hawai'i is the Balinese influence. Beginning in the late 1980s, the trend has steamrolled through the Islands, perhaps because it suits Hawai'i so well.

The Balinese look, with its honed and natural surfaces and playful attitude, has been the subject of several international design books. Well made of natural woods, and well priced, the style has become the natural choice for both Islanders and mainlanders with vacation homes. Travel to Bali is popular and regular, and this fuels the affinity.

There is a strong sense of freedom in the use of materials and the elimination of polished surfaces. The Balinese style is the epitome of a "rooms without walls" lifestyle; the rustic pieces move seamlessly between indoors and out.

Indonesia is extremely hot and humid, and there is a need for surfaces that appear cool. This has led to the use of water and water gardens everywhere. The surfaces of vessels filled with water create refreshing planes. It is truly a sensory approach to design.

Hawaiian designers are expert at taking the earthy, elemental quality of Balinese objects and "making them Hawaiian." It's a very good fit.

Opposite: A Balinese carving makes a dramatic accent on this outside wall.

Below: This Big Island home was designed by architect Mark de Reus to take advantage of the warm, dry weather. Interior design is by Mary Philpotts.

Above and opposite: Interior designer Mary Philpotts has taken the owners' love of color and infused this oceanside home with great warmth. Their favorite shades of coral, gold, green, and periwinkle have been used inside and out on the plaster walls. Then lime green, coral reds, teal, and lavender were used as accents. An antique green Chinese lacquer table in the center of the room is a cheery attention-getter. The owners wanted their home to be playful, happy, and casual. The interior sculptures (right) come off Indonesian fence posts. The designer mounted them on old black house columns, and then had several other figures installed in the garden outside.

CUTTING-EDGE CRAFTSMANSHIP

If there ever was an exercise in home-building that stretched crafts-men to their limits, this was it. Everything about the house is non-traditional. Designed to the elements, and to take advantage of the extraordinary Island light by cutting shapes into ceilings and walls and filling them with colored glass, the home takes a totally new look at the idea of a "sense of place."

New York artistic director Christopher Janney and interior design-er Holly Boling Ruiz of Philpotts & Associates kept the colors vivid to give the spaces a feeling of richness and simplicity. The bold fur-niture was designed by Janney and made by the Honolulu firm of Martin & MacArthur, with inspiration taken from the geometric shapes in Polynesian tattoos and kapa. The house is a blending of handmade objects and technology.

Everything about the place speaks to the senses and is oriented to enjoy the ocean and the night sky. Built around a central open courtyard, the house also has an observatory deck from which to view the stars. Rooms flow from the inside out and back in again, almost without your knowing.

Opposite: Shutters pull back to the walls to allow the outside in.

Top: The wine cellar was made to look like the inside of a lava tube, complete with a saltwater aquarium fed by ocean water. The architect was Robert Nespor.

Above: Christopher Janney custom-designed this sofa and back table. It was then made in teak by Martin & MacArthur especially for the house.

Left: The Janney-designed table with a chevron-patterned top was made for the home by Martin & MacArthur.

Top left: An Indonesian offering bowl filled with coral from the beach outside.

Top right: A black-and-white Hawaiian quilt tops a bed of bird's eye maple. It is essentially a pūne'e with a built-in headboard. The night stands have sound windows cut into the front which pipe in the sounds of the ocean each night.

Right: The rock wall was cut with stones in the same patterns that were used throughout the house's interior.

Opposite: The stepped cabinets in one corner of the bedroom were designed by Holly Boling Ruiz and inspired by Japanese tansu. They serve as a closet, television cabinet, and dresser. The piece was made of mahogany by Martin & MacArthur. The big bamboo chair and ottoman are for lounging.

If I look through the curtains

of leaves hanging down

I can see tiny glimmers of dazzling blue

And patches of turquoise and blotches of brown

With spatters of yellow

And orange and mellow;

The sea and the sky and the roofs of the town.

From *Vagabond's House* by Don Blanding

A Closer Look

The Island aesthetic is achieved bit by bit by the layering of veiled light through shutters, sudari blinds, or sheer curtains, and the application of tropical colors and local art. Collections, flowers, and everyday found items all mix to create homes that are quintessentially Hawaiian. We let you get in close and observe. You may want to take their lead and extract some ideas for yourself.

VEILED LIGHT

As surprising as it may seem, the outdoor light in Hawai'i can be fatiguing. Those Victorian and plantation residences built in the late 19th and early 20th century had dark, restful interiors that made everything seem cooler. The furniture was natural wood or wicker; on the floors of Island woods or stained concrete were Oriental rugs and lauhala mats. Usually, there were cooling ferns and oversized tropical flowers—bunches of ginger, heliconia, ti, and palms—often stuck into a collection of precious and utilitarian containers.

Hawai'i homes had larger and traditionally less uniform window shapes than homes in cooler climates. It is rare to find heavily swagged windows and fabric-covered valances, because they simply look out of place and don't fare well unless the environment is air-conditioned. Yet there is the need to address the too bright, restless light.

Shutters, though expensive, are one good solution because they allow the control of ventilation, block inclement weather, and don't bang annoyingly in the wind at night. When drapery is used, it is best that it be sheer or open-weave, allowing the air through.

Cross-ventilation is always an issue. Old-fashioned café or half curtains have been around forever, because they are successful in this climate, offering privacy, while allowing light and air to circulate. Usually washable, they make a good choice for children's rooms.

Sudari blinds are another solution to bring down the level of light, while allowing you to see outside. They have both an exotic and natural appearance. During the day, they let the air through, still protecting fabrics, wood, and walls from the damaging rays of the sun.

Sudari blinds have one big disadvantage. They create a fishbowl effect at night when the lights are on. If this is an issue, a combination of drapery or roller shades can solve the problem. There are many good sudari look-a-likes on the market today that simulate the look of grasses and natural fibers.

Right: Afternoon sun is veiled through slanted wood blinds in this contemporary dining room designed by Marion Philpotts Miller and Kaui Philpotts.

Below: Textured sudari-style blinds roll down to allow light, while also providing privacy during the daytime.

Opposite: The roll-up textured shades create a soft light and ambiance in this dining space. The batik painting on the wall is by artist Yvonne Cheng. The round koa table by Island artisan McD Philpotts reflects an older woodcraft tradition, while new wicker chairs update the look. Interior design by Mary Philpotts.

Opposite: Sheer curtains give privacy, while allowing cool breezes and light into this massage area at a Big Island resort.

Above: Traditional Japanese shoji screens veil the light in this bedroom. Architect Vladimir Ossipoff used shoji screens and natural redwood walls in many of his mid-century homes. The oil painting is by artist Alan Leitner. Interior design by Kaui Philpotts.

Below: Multiple light sources, from indoor lighting and the city outside, give this room a soft and romantic nighttime atmosphere. Interior design by Marion Philpotts Miller.

JUST COLOR

Most people are automatically drawn to a definite color palette that works for them. If you do the exercise of going through magazines and books, you will be better able to see your levels of tolerance and intolerance for strong color.

There is a natural tendency to select colors that work with your own coloring. While this may seem like a sweeping generalization, dark-haired, dark-eyed people tend to like more saturated color. More often fair-haired people will select delicate colors in the celadon or raspberry families. Children can live with much more intense color than their parents. In warm climates like Mexico and India the use of brilliant color is part of everyday life.

Lots of color works especially well in small areas where you don't spend a lot of time. The powder room is a good example. These little rooms can have unexpected finesse in their use of color, pattern, and texture. If you have one, and are afraid of strong color elsewhere, it's a good place to start. If you don't like it, you can easily paint it again.

Hawaiian color tends to be rich and saturated, as seen in the quilts, bold fabrics, and bark-cloth designs. This color is often balanced with earthy, natural textures and hues from koa, teak, or monkey pod, and grasses in mats and window treatments. Earthy and natural tones are more restful and timeless. Unlike the 1920s through the 1950s, bathrooms and kitchens now tend to be more neutral, because they are costly to renovate, and there is the consideration of the home's resale value.

One very effective way to use deep color is in a room that is broken up with moldings, trims, and many apertures such as doors and windows. Using color can help bring all the parts together into a whole and creates an interesting composition. When the molding and trims are left neutral there is relief from too much color while giving structure and identity to the detailing. It also helps to reduce the light level and make the room more restful.

Opposite: Interior designer Marion Philpotts Miller infused this child's room with brilliant color by painting one wall a vivid pink and placing a colorful and graphic covering on the bed. The hanging Chinese lanterns give the room a further edge.

Below: A collection of Asian puppets add color and interest to a room's corner.

Opposite: Designer Marion Philpotts Miller found this long farm table in Napa Valley and surrounded it with inherited European-style dining chairs. She punched up the color of the walls by taking a cue from wall art she assembled from bits of bright carpet.

Top left: The bright yellow wall accentuates the Mexican painting, a flea-market find, and sets off the Japanese paper lamp and vintage figurine on a nearby table.

Top right: The marquetry woodwork and bird of paradise design handpainted by Georg James and John Dinsmore make this end table stand out with vivid color.

Below left: Brilliant croton leaves from a front-yard hedge echo the colors used in the interiors on this page.

Above: A patterned indigo-and-cream chair and cushions, Oriental rug, and Chinese ceramic pedestal stool combine to make a powder room elegant and inviting.

Right: Blue plastered walls set the tone for this cozy vignette. The trunk is a 19th century Dutch sea trunk from Indonesia, and the vintage painting is a 1930s flea-market find. Interior design by Jonathan Staub.

Opposite: Indonesian batik hangers and hand-printed Southeast Asian fabrics sewn together make for a dramatic wall piece behind the blue-and-white beds in this bedroom.

Right: The vibrant pinks and blues of the flowers in the foreground enhance the large painting on the patio beyond.

Opposite: A showstopping piece of multicolored glass sculpture adds excitement to this countertop. The interior design is by Mary Philpotts and Shawn Moynahan.

Following pages: Simple natural objects become art when displayed prominently in the home.

USING ART AND SCULPTURE

Sources of artwork for the home are endless. It can be something as precious as a framed oil by a beloved regional artist such as Madge Tennent or D. Howard Hitchcock, or as ordinary as green coconuts placed all in a row.

Art really is in the eye of the beholder. Mural-painted walls and trompe l'oeil on furniture can be very effective in adding a sense of place. Architects like C. W. Dickey and Hart Wood often used Hawaiian and Asian motifs incorporated into the design of their buildings through window openings and arches. A room should be treated as you would a painting. There should be areas to excite the eye balanced by areas that let the eye rest. As an example, a large, brilliant oil painting needs to be relieved on another wall by something quieter such as simply framed black-and-white photographs. Don't be afraid to go from "positive to negative." Vary the size and type of art you incorporate into your rooms to layer and give interest. Group smaller objects together to create one larger form.

Look for good traditional art and local handicrafts such as kapa cloth, or even a collection of smooth river stones. Papier-mâché masks make a dramatic wall, as can old maps or pretty fans. They add a sense of whimsy and humor.

Opposite: The owners of this home are fervent art lovers and certainly not afraid to use color. The large oil painting entitled "Mayonnaise Window" is by Christopher Brown. The sculpture in the corner is by Stephan Balkenhol. The 1930s home was built by one-time C. Brewer executive David Larsen. Interior design is by Jonathan Staub.

Above left: The trunk of an old banyan is a piece of nature's art.

Above right: The abstract bronze horse grazing on this Honolulu lawn is by Montana-based sculptor Deborah Butterfield.

Left: The colorful love seat under the shade of a tree is by artist Gordon Chandier.

Opposite: The carved tiki posts by Tom Pico become part of the interior architecture of this Big Island home designed by architect Shay Zak. The interiors are by Mary Philpotts.

Top: The framed Polynesian kapa is approximately 100 years old and is believed to have been used by women in ceremonies. Squatted below is a Philippine rice god, traditionally carved by young boys.

Below: Male and female tiki figures by contemporary artist Tom Pico stand tall at the entrance to this Big Island residence.

COLLECTIONS AND VIGNETTES

Hawaiian style has always been about things being "passed down." Objects with a well-worn patina say comfort, respect, and familiarity. Even old rattan, once purchased only for the family room and lānai, is treasured today. But whether you were lucky enough to come from one of these families or not, collections that inspire you can become an important part of your room design.

Collections don't always have to be highly priced. Often it's the less serious ones that are the freshest and most amusing.

Begin with anything you love, from beach glass to shell lei. Whatever you decide to collect, be discriminating. The best collections are the ones selected piece by piece by the collector himself. This is a sure way to create value.

Become educated about the objects you choose to collect. It will help you discriminate and make it easier to cull items when you feel your collection is getting too large. Collecting is also a wonderful way to enhance your trips. There's nothing like the thrill of the hunt away from home.

Once you've determined you have a collection, you will want to display it. Items scattered about your home don't have nearly the impact they would if you massed them together or presented them in groups.

Consider how others will see your collection. Many people collect tiny boxes, for example. The best way to view boxes is by looking down on them to see their colorful and intricate covers. Does your collection need a dark or light background? The arrangement itself becomes part of the impact of a collection.

Opposite: A collection of hula girls sits atop a cabinet believed to have been designed by Walter Lamb. The floral painting is by Island artist Frank Oda. The designer is Mary Philpotts.

Top: An antique Chinese cabinet holds old calabashes of Hawaiian woods. The paintings are by Madge Tennent. The small lacquer cabinet is Japanese.

Below: A charming collection of frogs clusters under a print by Island artist Lloyd Sexton.

Opposite: Bowls of coconut and Hawaiian woods are displayed prominently in this Island library bookcase. Design by Mary Philpotts.

Top: A Hawaiian stone squid weight and fish-hooks makes a casual and effective tabletop display.

Below left: The owner's collection of shell lei, many from the Island of Ni'ihau, drapes luxuriously over a calabash.

Below right: This ancient Hawaiian feather cloak and rare Ni'ihau shell lei are from a private collection.

Above: This Asian vignette effectively juxtaposes the painting of horses with the Chinese seated figure and horse and iron pot.

Opposite: The owner's sense of humor and whimsy are apparent in this collection of Chinese cricket cages of all sizes.

Next two pages: This cabinet was painted to look like a Japanese tansu filled with treasures by artists Georg James and John Dinsmore. The pair enjoy taking castoff pieces and decorating them with paint to look grander than they are. The owner's collectibles are arranged on top. Interiors by Rici Guild Conger and Alice Guild.

Handmade slippers, Chinese ceramic fruit, and smooth pebbles make an interesting display on this chow table. The stool once belonged to a shopkeeper in China.

Above left: A collection of floral frogs makes a pleasing display in this wire rack.

Above right: A tiny Thai spirit house is nestled onto a branch in this garden corner.

Opposite: Indonesian garden sculptures of ceremonial musicians from a gamelan band add interest to this cluster of water-garden pots.

Right and below: Collections of mid-century kitsch from Hula Heaven on the Kona Coast. These charming items, once made as inexpensive souvenirs, are now highly collectible.

Top: Monkeys, vintage ceramic leaf plates from Hula Heaven, and beaded Indonesian boxes all make interesting tabletop groupings.

Left: An Island kitchen cabinet filled with the owner's collection of brightly colored painted Chinese serving dishes. Once regularly used in homes and restaurants, the dishes are now collector's items.

I hope that I can make you see

This sunlit, moon-witched, rainbow place

Of beauty. Just a little space

Quite filled with flowers, vines and trees,

Walled in with stone, the haunt of bees

And butterflies and lunar moths.

When you are passing will you pause

Or – if you will – drop in and see

This garden that belongs to me.

From "In an Old Hawaiian Garden" by Don Blanding

CELEBRATIONS

Drop in and see how we do it. Islanders love to eat and drink. Entertaining is more often

done in homes, or even beach parks, than in fine-dining restaurants. In fact, having just

enough to go around is not the Hawaiian way. Like the interiors of our homes, we mix it

all up—Hawaiian kālua pork, Japanese sushi, Chinese noodles, Korean barbecue, Filipino

bibingka, and German beer all at one feast. We love our families, and we love our friends.

There is no better place to put all these elements together than at an Island wedding.

A Garden Wedding

While a garden in Hawai'i is considered tropical, because of the many microclimates within the Islands, it can be extremely varied. A garden in the cool, uplands of Kula or Waimea, for instance, will be vastly different from the rocky, dry Kohala Coast. Many plants labeled tropical will only survive near the windy and salty seashore. The brilliantly colored bougainvillea, for example, is happiest in dry, hot areas, as is the common plumeria, often called the "graveyard flower," because of its tolerance for neglect.

Because Hawai'i's climate experiences only minor changes during the year (cooler and wetter November through March), gardens are frequently used as outdoor rooms. People enjoy sitting and entertaining in their yards and on their lānai.

There is a "chop suey," or mixed-up cottage quality to many Island gardens, born perhaps from the days of Island plantation and ranch living. Neighbors readily shared cuttings with each other and gave gardening advice. Until recently, Island residents rarely used landscape architects; their gardens grew as their interests did—by looking at other gardens and perusing nurseries and garden shops.

Today there is an important influence from Southeast Asia with large ceramic pots and stone vessels. Water features have always been important. They can be as elaborate as a large pond filled with koi, or as simple as a pot with lotus or black taro.

There is also a lot of layering. Trees, for example, will have honohono orchids or tree ferns attached to them. Hinahina, or Spanish moss, drops from branches of plumeria trees. Many plant for their tabletops and the lei they make. Bromeliads, a fairly new introduction into the Island garden, are used to add color and drama. Coupled with balmy nights and sweet scents, the result is overwhelmingly romantic and exotic.

Preceding pages: A garden urn bursts with an array of tropical flowers. A tent with a transparent top and shell chandeliers is filled with lūa'u tables and colorful pastel linens at this wedding feast in a family's garden.

Above left: A tiered wedding cake with a Polynesian kapa design that was created by the bride and groom.

Above right: A wedding takes place in an Island streambed while guests and members of a Tahitian dance group watch from the banks.

Right: Tent poles have been decorated with tropical foliage, flowers and sea shells by designers Georg James and John Dinsmore.

Opposite: A wedding lūa'u tabletop with brightly patterned Tahitian pareu prints and tropical flowers in a coconut vase. The pineapple, green onions, and 'alaea salt accompany the lūa'u food.

Holo i'a ka papa, kau 'ia oe ka manu.

Where there is food, people gather.
(Hawaiian proverb)

Right: Ornate columns of white crown flower and fragrant maile create an aisle for the bride and groom at the Henderson-Chillingworth wedding on the Big Island. Floral decorations were created by popular designer Ernest Parker.

Below: Helen Henderson and Sheldon "Buddy" Chillingworth are shown at their 1939 wedding at the bride's home Moanike'ala, near Hilo. The couple are surrounded by strands of white crown flower and ti leaves. The bride wears the traditional holokū of white satin.

Top: Flexible bamboo poles with baskets bursting with scented yellow plumeria blossoms and monstera leaves decorate the setting for this garden wedding on O'ahu.

Left: A detail of the plumeria and monstera baskets.

'Owe sanana

Make merry.
(Hawaiian proverb)

DINING HAWAIIAN STYLE

Hawaiian hospitality has never been about keeping up appearances or showing off. Like the best entertaining anywhere in the world, it concerns itself with providing comfort, simplicity, and enjoyment to the guest.

It means setting a table for a poi supper, or even take-out Chinese food, with the best you own. Forget about those matching sets of silver flatware—use what you have and fill in with whatever suits your fancy. In the mid-20th century, monkey pod wood trays became popular with many Islanders.

Together with woven lauhala placemats and arrangements of flowers and fruit assembled from the backyard, or the local supermarket, the look is complete.

The traditional poi supper includes kālua pig, laulau (meat or fish and taro leaves steamed in ti leaves), lomilomi salmon, baked bananas or sweet potatoes, and maybe chicken with long rice (cellophane noodles). It's finished off with haupia or coconut cake and lots of beer and whiskey.

But the poi supper is not the only typical kamaʻāina meal. Islanders draw shamelessly from all cultures. Just as "local" are curry dinners, Japanese-inspired chicken or beef hekka prepared in a wok, kalbi ribs on a beach grill, and Hawaiian stew and rice.

Previous pages: Two tables are set in the Island style. Wooden plates and bowls will hold dishes for a traditional poi supper. The placemats are made of woven lauhala, and the arrangement of garden leaves, anthuriums, and fresh fruit creates a tropical cornucopia. A vintage tablecloth, Lokelani china, garden leaves, and a bowl of fresh papayas are a pleasing setting for an afternoon lunch.

Above: A Balinese pavilion placed in a Honolulu garden designed by Mary Philpotts and landscape consultant Leland Miyano lights up the evening hours.

Top right: A garden gazebo surrounded by large hāpu'u ferns and lush foliage in the Henderson family garden near Hilo on the Big Island, circa 1934.

Right: A garden at "Niniko," the Honolulu home of Frederick J. Lowrey.

Opposite: A youthful and amusing take on a traditional Island table. Old-fashioned grass hula skirts act as a table skirt with a tabletop of batik-patterned fabric. The hostess has taken advantage of in-season gardenias and placed them randomly about the table in bamboo and water glasses. Banana leaves have been used as placemats and ti leaves adorn the sconces.

TABLETOPS

Islanders follow many of the same trends as people elsewhere. Having said that, there are traditions that are uniquely Hawaiian. They party and entertain more in their homes and yards than most. This applies to all areas of Island society, from the picnic tables in carports in Waimānalo to the lānai along the golf course at Wai'alae Kāhala. The best incorporate table décor and food reflective of their culture as well as current fashion.

A mother may decorate her table with a voluptuous arrangement of waxy, tropical leaves and heliconia, while her daughter's minimal tastes have her placing single, slender-stemmed red anthuriums in clear glass bottles down the length of her table.

In the 1930s, wooden plates and bowls made of monkey pod wood became very popular. They were inexpensive and ideal for parties where you served chicken curry and for traditional poi suppers. They are large and sturdy and still used in many households.

Canton china in the rose medallion motif was another kama'āina favorite. These colorful, intricately handpainted dishes have been handed down for generations and are now quite expensive collector's pieces. They make a table much more formal than the wooden plates.

Rare and lovely Lokelani china was first used by haole and Hawaiian families in the 1890s as everyday or "kitchen china." It was strong and had several large rose-like flowers with leaves connected into a wreath pattern around the rim. A set was first given as a wedding gift to the son of a missionary who married an Englishwoman whose father owned a pottery business in Staffordshire. The business was eventually sold to Royal Doulton.

Lokelani china has been made by several companies including George Jones & Sons, Ltd., Crescent (G.J. & Sons) in Staffordshire, Societe Ceramique Maestricht (Holland), and W.W. Dimond & Co., Ltd. (Honolulu). Lokelani began as everyday china, but is now highly desirable and handed down or hunted for in yard sales and flea markets.

Opposite: Old and new table settings contrast, yet speak the same language—informality and the use of Asian and natural elements. Often flowers and leaves from the garden are combined to make striking table arrangements. Old Japanese obi and lauhala placemats work equally well when setting a table.

This page bottom: A detail of Lokelani china made by the Dutch company, Societe Ceramique Maestricht, and found in an Indonesian roadside market.

Vintage settings are from the old Fagan home, photographed in the 1930s. Current settings are by Mary Philpotts, Alice Guild, and Kaui Philpotts.

NA LEI

The importance of the fresh flower lei in celebrations of all kinds is evident everywhere, from graduations and birthdays to weddings and anniversaries. Lei are given for any and all occasions. When a building is blessed, maile is untied at the entrance. There are lei especially appropriate for just men, for women, and even for children. When the event has passed, Islanders have a hard time letting them go. You will find them dried on bedposts, draped around mirrors and calabashes, and flung on doorknobs—a constant reminder of affection and an event where everyone probably had a very good time.

Right: Days-old orchid lei tossed around the neck of a reproduction of a Chinese terra cotta warrior on an outdoor patio.

Opposite: A collection of dried flower lei are tossed over an enormous Hawaiian calabash. Sudari blinds veil the light in the room. The abstract painting is by the owner.

ACKNOWLEDGMENTS

A book comes together bit by bit, photo by photo, and in the end there are so many people to thank—those who have lent their talent and creativity to tell our story. Our first string, indispensable team was Lloyd Jones of Martin & MacArthur, Kaui Philpotts, Cindy Turner, and Hi'ilei Dye. A special thanks to the hardworking designers and staff at Philpotts & Associates—Marion Philpotts Miller, Jonathan Staub, Lowell Tom, Holly Boling Ruiz, Belinda Akaka, Heidi Hennessey, Gerri Pedesky, and Kelly Pierce, and to the generous, stylish people who allowed us to come into their homes and photograph their most inspirational spaces.

I would like to recognize the innovative architects whose rooms our firm has helped enhance. Among them are David Stringer, Philip "Pip" White, Geoffrey Lewis, Shay Zak, Mark de Reus, John Hara, Kurt Mitchell, Tan Hock Beng, Sidney Snyder, Warren Sunnland, Christopher Janney, Robert Nespor, and all the architects before them who created our unique Island style and whose legacies are featured in this book.

David Duncan Livingston was with us from the beginning with his sensitive and lively photographs. David Franzen stepped in with additional shots at the last minute. I am grateful for the work of Linny Morris Cunningham, Peter French, Kelvin Nakano, Mary E. Nichols, Cindy Turner, and all the others who allowed the use of their photos.

A big mahalo to Dr. Bill Brown, Dr. Tim Choy, Betty Tatar, and DeSoto Brown at the Bishop Museum who allowed us to spend hours in the photo archives picking through vintage photos of Island homes, and for their generosity in letting us use them in this book.

Georg James and John Dinsmore provided wonderful drawings and their talented designs have enhanced many a wall and piece of furniture in these lovely homes. McD Philpotts has, with his skilled craftsmanship and Island spirit, created furniture that rises to the level of art.

I would also like to thank Jon Martin, Barbara Rodrigues, Miller Fong, Irving Jenkins, Bob Dye, my sisters Alice Guild and Judith Flanders, their husbands Robert Guild and James D. Staub, Rici Guild Conger, Helen Chillingworth, Alison Bhattacharyya, Mark deMello, Roberta B. Bialek, Martin and Margaret Brauns, Jack and Carol Briggs, Dennis and Susie Fitzgerald, George and Nancy Ellis, Mark and Diane Hastert, Jeannette and Grant Heidrich, Gwen and Evan Olins of Hula Heaven, Judie and Richard Malmgren, Kathy Merrill, Doug and Kaui Philpotts, Valley and Phil Reilly, John Ryan, Heidi Snow, Nakila and Marti Steele, Claudia Herfurt, David and Karen Wegmann, Dominique Fraikin, Shawn Moynahan, Joan Moynahan, Moloka'i Ranch Lodge; Moloka'i Properties, Ltd., Dowling Company, Inc., Colony Capital, LLC, Jeffrey Miller, David Cheever, Mary Richards, Phyllis Spalding, and Mary Kimball.

Mary Philpotts McGrath

Left: Islanders, fearful of rain and bad weather before an important event, will put out an offering of gin on a ti leaf as an appeasement to higher powers. It's not clear when this began, but there are those who swear by it.

BIBLIOGRAPHY

Blackburn, Mark. *Hawaiiana: The Best of Hawaiian Design*. Atglen, Pa.: Schiffer Publishing, Ltd., 1996.

Blanding, Don. *Vagabond's House*. New York: Dodd, Mead & Co., 1928.

Bryant, Chris and Paige Gilchrist. *The New Book of Table Settings*. New York: Lark Books, 2000.

Craft, Mabel. *Hawaii Nei*. San Francisco: William Doxey at the Sign of the Lark, 1899.

Department of Land and Natural Resources, "Hawaiian Style Cottages." State Historic Preservation Division, State of Hawai'i, 1995.

Fairfax, Geoffrey W. *The Architecture of Honolulu*. Honolulu: Island Heritage, Ltd., 1971.

Grierson, Mary and Peter S. Green. *A Hawaiian Florilegium*. Lawai, Kauai, Hawai'i: National Tropical Botanical Garden, 1996.

Hawai'i State Preservation Office. "Oral Histories of 1930s Architects." Department of Land and Natural Resources, September 1982.

Holoholo Honolulu. "C. Brewer Building is Like Home." *Honolulu Star-Bulletin*, September 28, 2003.

Jenkins, Irving. *Hawaiian Furniture and Hawaii's Cabinetmakers*. Honolulu: Editions Limited, 1983.

Pukui, Mary Kawena. *Olelo Noeau*. Honolulu: Bishop Museum Press, 1983.

Schwartz, Harvey. *Rattan: Tropical Comfort throughout the House*. Atglen, Pa.: Schiffer Publishing, Ltd. 1999.

Seckel, Harry W. *Hawaiian Residential Architecture*. Honolulu: Bishop Museum Press, 1954.

Severson, Don R., Michael D. Horikawa, and Jennifer Saville. *Finding Paradise*. Honolulu Academy of Arts, Honolulu: University of Hawai'i Press, 2002.

Stall, Edna Williamson. *Historic Homes of Hawai'i: From Clipper Ship to Clipper Ship*. New York: Privately printed, 1937.

Warren, William. *The Tropical Garden*. London, England: Thames & Hudson Inc. 1991.

Williams-Sonoma. *Entertaining*. Menlo Park, Ca.: Oxmoor House, 2004.

PHOTO CREDITS

INDEX